Cynthia

RICH: NUGENTS *Cynthia.*

CONTAINING

Direfull Sonnets, Madrigalls, and paſsionate intercourſes, deſcribing *his repudiate affections expreſſed* in Loues owne Language.

Non ad imitandum, ſed ad precauendum.

Diſce ex me.

LONDON

Printed by T. P. for Henrie Tomes, and are to be ſould at his ſhop by Graies Inne new gate in *Holborne.* 1604.

CYNTHIA

by Richard Nugent

edited by
Angelina Lynch

with an introductory essay by
Anne Fogarty

FOUR COURTS PRESS

Set in 10.5 pt on 13 pt Bembo for
FOUR COURTS PRESS LTD
7 Malpas Street, Dublin 8, Ireland
www.fourcourtspress.ie
and in North America for
FOUR COURTS PRESS
c/o ISBS, 920 N.E. 58th Avenue, Suite 300, Portland, OR 97213.

A catalogue record for this title
is available from the British Library.

ISBN 978-1-84682-107-3

Printed in England
by CPI Antony Rowe, Chippenham, Wilts.

Contents

Preface 7
Acknowledgments 8
Introduction *by Anne Fogarty* 9
A note on the text 46

CYNTHIA

Epigraph 48
Dedicatory Sonnet 49
The First Part 51
The Second Part 66
The Third Part 77

The Literature of Early Modern Ireland series

Previously published in the series:
Faithful Teate's *Ter Tria* ed. and introduced by Angelina Lynch (2007)
Henry Burkhead's *Cola's Furie* ed. Angelina Lynch with an introductory essay by Patricia Coughlan (2009)

Forthcoming volumes in the series:
William Dunkin's *The Parson's Revels* (*c*.1745) ed. and introduced by Katie Skeen
The anonymous *Vertue Rewarded; or, The Irish Princess* (1693) ed. Ian Campbell Ross and Anne Markey

Preface

This series of editions of English-language texts from seventeenth- and eighteenth-century Ireland has been undertaken in the belief that the study of Early Modern Ireland is in a new and exciting phase. As thousands of web-based images of English-language texts from Early Modern Ireland have become available to scholars and students during the last few years (through 'Early English Books Online' and the 'Eighteenth Century Collections Online' for instance), so the necessity for authoritative editions of key texts has become ever more acute. Interest in Early Modern Ireland is constantly increasing and what is needed now is a series of definitive editions of some key literary and dramatic texts, edited to the highest standards and set into context by scholars and editors of international standing; such is this series.

The series was originally conceived as one which would embrace verse and drama before embarking on the rather more substantial prose texts of the period. However recent developments have led to a very welcome arrangement by which a series of prose fictions (*c.*1680–*c.*1820), under the editorship of Professor Ian Campbell Ross of Trinity College Dublin, Dr Aileen Douglas of Trinity College Dublin and Dr Moyra Haslett of Queen's University Belfast, will appear alongside the verse and drama texts originally envisaged.

Meanwhile, our particular thanks go to Dr Angelina Lynch who has worked enthusiastically and tirelessly on the editorial side of this project for the last three years.

Andrew Carpenter
General Editor
Dublin, May 2009

Acknowledgments

We are very grateful to Professor Anne Fogarty for providing the introduction for this book.

The editorial work for this volume could not have been brought to completion without the award of an IRCHSS (Irish Research Council for the Humanities and Social Sciences) post-doctoral fellowship to Dr Angelina Lynch. We are grateful to the Council for its support of this project and to the UCD School of English, Drama and Film for hosting Dr Lynch during her fellowship.

We also acknowledge with thanks a grant to aid towards the costs of publication from the National University of Ireland.

Thanks are due also to the libraries of University College Dublin, Trinity College Dublin, the National Library of Ireland, the British Library and the Huntington Library, San Marino, California. Martin Fanning and the team at Four Courts Press have been supportive and helpful in bringing the book into existence.

Angelina Lynch would also like to thank Andrew Carpenter for his support and encouragement.

Introduction

Anne Fogarty

Richard Nugent's *Cynthia containing direfull sonnets, madrigalls, and passionate intercourses, describing his repudiate affections expressed in love's owne language* was published by Thomas Purfoot for Henry Tomes in London in 1604.[1] As with many works from early modern Ireland, few exemplars of this slim volume survive whether due to the chronic political instability of the country or the limited numbers of texts originally produced.[2] Of the two extant copies, which are identical, one is housed in the British Library in London and the other is held in the Huntington Library in California. Despite its brevity, *Cynthia* unusually is divided into three parts: Part I contains nineteen sonnets, followed by five madrigals and a ballata; Part II consists of thirteen sonnets interspersed with a canzone and two madrigals; Part III features an epistolary exchange of six sonnets between named friends and relations of Nugent to which two sonnets are appended. The penultimate renunciatory sonnet is apparently in the author's voice, but the final poem, which is in Italian, may be an intervention by another writer.

As the first sonnet sequence in English by an Irishman, *Cynthia* is a unique document and of signal cultural and historical importance. Yet its manifest resonance is matched in equal measure by its cryptic qualities. It is necessarily elusive because it draws on the heavily coded rhetoric of the Renaissance sonnet sequence. Such poetry is designed for subterfuge as much as for affective public display. The posturings of sonnets never conveniently yield trustworthy biographical information about the writer and his intent, nor do they allow us easily to adduce social and historical contexts.

1 I have incurred many debts in writing this Introduction. I would like to thank Andrew Carpenter, Fionnán Tuite, Thomas Herron, Vincent Carey and Gerald Power for generously sharing their ideas. I am especially grateful to Angelina Lynch for her intellectual guidance and the numerous instructive discussions which have played a material role in shaping the arguments here.

2 On the history of reading and book production and the socio-economics of literary culture in early modern Ireland, see Raymond Gillespie, *Reading Ireland: print, reading and social change in early modern Ireland* (Manchester, 2005), and Andrew Carpenter, 'Literature in print, 1550–1800' in Raymond Gillespie and Andrew Hadfield (eds), *The Oxford history of the Irish book. Volume III: The Irish book in English, 1550–1800* (Oxford, 2006), pp 301–18.

However, beyond this, *Cynthia* is enigmatic for numerous other reasons. Many facets of its authorship, provenance, composition history, putative audience, symbolic structures and discreetly masked political subtexts are uncertain and raise challenging questions for the literary scholar and the Renaissance historian alike. These questions may be canvassed and debated but not all of them can fully or satisfactorily be answered. This essay seeks to outline these interpretive cruxes, to outline what can currently be established with certainty about Richard Nugent and his milieu and to propose ways in which his text might be framed and interpreted.

My aim will be not only to assemble as much as can be ascertained reliably about this shadowy author, but also to sift through suggestive details that allow us to build up plausible inferences about his life and work. In particular, the structures and intertextuality of Nugent's sonnet cycle permit us to get a measure of his learning and to pinpoint his literary ambitions and the particular purchase and weight of the chief tropes that he deploys. Such an investigation also allows us an appreciation of his ability to make his own of Petrarchan and counter-Petrarchan conventions and to use the power games of amatory verse to adumbrate the political issues that vexed the Old English community in late sixteenth-century Ireland, and to give these predicaments a symbolic form and impress. Further, several critical perspectives on these sonnets will be offered to illustrate their multi-faceted nature and to signpost pathways for future readers and scholars.

Above all, it will be argued that *Cynthia* has been inexplicably neglected. It invites further scrutiny and has unjustly been consigned to oblivion in the manner of many other sonnet sequences that have been deemed to be minor and hence relegated from the canon. As will become apparent, it is of moment because it offers a variety of conflicting but instructive insights into the cultural politics of the Old English community in Tudor Ireland and because it is a subtle and purposeful remoulding of a key Renaissance literary form – the sonnet sequence – by an accomplished artist for personal, political, aesthetic and tactical purposes. The ligatures between local, national and transnational allegiances and the intertwining of variable webs of reference are marshalled by Nugent to represent the thwarted and divided loyalties of the Old English in Ireland at the turn of the seventeenth century. Above all, the controlled artistry and unembellished style of his work warrant attention and need to be probed to uncover a playful intricacy as well as an original recasting of the formal structures and affective metaphors of the sonnet cycle. With these goals in mind, in this introduction I shall consider *Cynthia* under the following aspects: I: authorship; II: The Old English and the problems of allegiance; III: The early modern sonnet sequence; IV: *Cynthia:* the poetics of intertextuality; V: Reading *Cynthia* politically.

I: AUTHORSHIP

The first intractable problem that faces readers of *Cynthia* is that of attribution. The contours of Nugent's biography are imprecise and hence vitiate firm identifications. Additionally, the fact that several members of the multiple branches of the Westmeath Nugent family bore the name of Richard and were roughly coeval further clouds matters. As a result, divergent identifications have been put forward by those historians and literary critics who have devoted attention to the provenance of this singular early modern sonnet sequence. The *Old Oxford dictionary of national biography* assigns a separate entry to Richard Nugent (fl. 1604). It identifies him as the son of Nicholas Nugent (d. 1582), comments that he received a 'good education', follows information in Lodge's *Peerage of Ireland* in recording that he inherited the family estate from his mother in 1615 and circumspectly notes that he was 'apparently' the author *Cynthia*.[3] In establishing this particular Richard Nugent as the writer of this text, a detailed rebuttal is given of a prior attribution to Richard Nugent, fifteenth baron Delvin and first earl of Westmeath, son of Christopher Nugent (1544–1602). The *New Oxford dictionary of national biography*, by and large, supports this late nineteenth-century identification but is likewise forced to acknowledge its tentative nature. Colm Lennon folds his brief biography of Richard Nugent into that of his father, Nicholas Nugent.[4] He gives his date of birth as 1564/5 and posits his death as having occurred in or after 1615. He describes Richard as an accomplished poet, but is still careful to specify that he is 'apparently' the author of *Cynthia*.[5]

By this reckoning, Richard Nugent was the heir to Nicholas and Ellen Nugent. His father, who trained at Lincoln's Inn, served the crown in Ireland in various legal and administrative capacities. He was appointed chief solicitor in 1566 and created second baron of the exchequer in 1570. Throughout the 1570s he was involved in the campaigns led by many of the chieftains in the Pale against cess, that is, arbitrary taxes imposed on landowners for the victualling of the English army in Ireland. He was twice imprisoned in Dublin Castle for his insubordination, and eventually stripped of his office by the lord deputy, Sir Henry Sidney. After Sidney's death he was appointed to the office of chief justice of the common pleas but this elevation was overturned through the machinations of his long-standing enemy, Robert Dillon. Nicholas Nugent's nephew, William Nugent, had mounted a campaign against the Crown protesting the imposition

3 *Old Oxford dictionary of national biography* (Oxford, 1894), p. 709. John Lodge, *The peerage of Ireland; or, A genealogical history of the present nobility of that kingdom collected from public records by John Lodge* (London, 1754), vol. 1, p. 132.

4 *New Oxford dictionary of national biography* (Oxford, 2006), pp 253–61.

5 Ibid., p. 261.

of cess; this had spilled over into armed rebellion by March 1581. Because of the close family connection, Nicholas Nugent was vulnerable to accusations of complicity. His enemies, including Robert Dillon, trumped up charges of conspiracy against him which they managed to have upheld despite scanty evidence. Nugent was hanged for treason on 6 April 1582. As Lennon attests, Richard Nugent, his son, had been taken hostage by the Irish privy council during the rebellion as a surety for the surrender of his cousin, son of the insurgent, William Nugent. He was later released on the payment of an indemnity. He married Anne, daughter of Christopher Rathfeigh, Co. Meath, and had at least one child. He succeeded his mother to the Nugent estate on 9 November 1615, but the duration of his tenure is unknown as is the date of his death.

Even though this Richard Nugent has customarily been held to be the author of *Cynthia*, internal evidence in the sonnet sequence itself appears to shed some doubt on this identification.[6] The final sonnet in Italian, that is appended to the cycle and written putatively by someone other than the originator of most of the preceding poems, announces that the writer has died. It is hence intimated that the text has been published posthumously. The author must as a consequence have passed away prior to the publication date of 1604. This scenario does not fit with the trajectory of Richard Nugent, son of Nicholas Nugent, who to all accounts survived into the second decade of the seventeenth century. Even though it would be feasible to read this belated announcement of the death of the author as a fictional ruse reinforcing the pathos routinely curried by the Renaissance lover, it is also plausible to read it as a factual intervention. Several early modern sonnet sequences were published after the death of their authors, including most famously that of Sir Philip Sidney. Such delayed publication may simply have been fortuitous. But it was also undoubtedly tied to the fact that such sequences were usually composed piecemeal and circulated initially in manuscript amongst a tight-knit coterie of friends and acquaintances. In addition, the somewhat dubious activity of sonneteering with its penchant for erotic themes and coded meanings leant itself to the guarded reading practices of a select and intimate audience. But as Marcy L. North cogently argues, it must also be borne in mind that sonnet sequences were usually written for publication and that coterie images within the cycles did not necessarily mean that the entire text circulated in manuscript.[7] It seems, then, the case that Nugent's sudden demise pre-

6 Historians who have upheld this identification include Basil Iske (Elisabeth Hickey) and Gerald Power. See Iske, *The green cockatrice* (Tara, 1978), p. 37 and Power, 'An expression of Old English identity: *Cynthia* (1604)', *History Studies* (University of Limerick History Society Journal) 7 (2006), 66–81.

7 Marcy L. North, 'The sonnets and book history' in Michael Schoenfeldt (ed.), *A companion to Shakespeare's sonnets* (Oxford, 2007), pp 204–21.

vented the publication of his text. Although *Cynthia* treats the deleterious nature of love and frequently depicts the poet-lover as longing for death, the declaration that the author has now died and that his beloved can also look forward to a heavenly reward and an end to her earthly suffering shockingly cuts across the rest of the cycle. The symbolic death faced by the repining Petrarchan lover is starkly displaced by actual mortality.

Albeit the demise of the author is skilfully and wittily woven into the texture of the sequence in this final, lone Italian sonnet and, as will later be shown, is made consonant with the themes of Petrarchanism, the possibility remains that its claims are at once genuine as well as poetic. Yet, it must also be acknowledged that the ambiguity of poetry and the playfulness of Petrarchan textuality do not permit us to extrapolate a definitive biography from the text. Like the unrequited love on which it centres, the death that concludes Nugent's sonnet sequence is on the one hand hypothetical and stylized, while on the other it is an integral part of the persuasive and affective narrative that is unfolded. Despite this undecidability, the unorthodox and startlingly dramatic ending of *Cynthia* does give pause and at the very least complicates our understanding of the notion of authorship underpinning this text and of its embedded themes.

A divergent but far less prominent strand of historical commentary has identified Richard Nugent (?1574 –?1604) as the son of the colourful insurgent figure, William Nugent (1550–1625).[8] William Nugent was the younger son of the Baron Delvin and an Oxford graduate. On the death of his father in 1559, he and his brother Christopher had become wards of the earl of Sussex, but probably received an early education with an Irish foster family. Nugent was known for his scholarship and composed poetry in Irish and in English. In his continuation of Holinshed's history of Ireland, Richard Stanihurst alludes to him in a section highlighting the learning and cultural accomplishments of the Old English community. He notes that he was 'a proper gentleman and of singuler good wit', adding that 'he wrote in the English tongue divers sonets'.[9] This account of William Nugent, however, merely profiles one aspect of his flamboyant personality and of his tempestuous and jagged career. His marriage took place in dramatic circumstances, as in 1573 he abducted Jane (or Janet) Marward, daughter of Walter Marward, Baron Skryne. Marward, who according to some

8 See, for example, Edwin B. Knowles, 'Thomas Shelton, translator of *Don Quixote*', *Studies in the Renaissance* 5 (1958), 160–75. Knowles explores the relationship between Richard Nugent, the son of William Nugent, and Thomas Shelton and notes that he is the author of *Cynthia* (p. 167).

9 See Liam Miller and Eileen Power (eds), *Holinshed's Irish chronicle: the historie of Ireland from the first inhabitation thereof, unto the yeare 1509*, collected by Raphaell Holinshed & continued till the yeare 1547 by Richard Stanyhurst (Dublin, 1979), p. 105.

sources was still a minor when she was seized by Nugent, had been betrothed by a relative of her mother, to Baron Dunsany.[10] But Nugent, in kidnapping her, was asserting his rights on the grounds of a prior marital arrangement that had supposedly been brokered by her stepfather, Nicholas Nugent. Marward became his wife in December 1573 and they had three children, the first of whom was Richard who was born *c.*1574. After the arrest of his brother, Christopher, and his brother-in-law, the earl of Kildare, in December 1580, Nugent was ineluctably drawn into the rebellion that had been fomented by the continuing campaigns against cess mounted by many Old English lords in the 1570s. He assembled an army and appears to have secured the release of his brother by early 1581, but remained in open opposition to the Dublin administration and the Crown. He sought alliances with several Gaelic chiefs, including the O'Connors and the O'Neills. By late 1581, the rebels were hard pressed as government reprisals took force, and many of the key insurgents were executed. Confederates of Nugent, amongst them his wife, were arrested and interrogated.

In January 1582, Nugent fled to Tyrone and departed from there to the Continent. In the succeeding years of exile, he sought assistance from the Catholic powers of Europe and, with this end in mind, spent an extended spell in Rome. He returned to Ireland in 1584 with a force of Scots supporters and allies and attempted to rally support from the Northern chiefs. However, after several clashes, he was forced to surrender to the Lord Deputy, Sir John Perrot. Remarkably, his insurgency did not result in ostracism or in punitive material loss. He was granted a pardon for his involvement in the 1584 uprising and his confiscated lands were officially restored to him in 1608. However, as Helen Coburn Walshe notes in her entry on William Nugent in the *New Oxford dictionary of national biography*, it is clear that he had access to them long before that date.[11] Throughout the 1590s he pursued a long-standing vendetta against the Dillons who had connived in the execution of his uncle, Nicholas Nugent, but he never managed to obtain the justice he sought. He died on 30 June 1625 without ever becoming involved in rebellious action again.

His oldest son, Richard, however, appears not only to have shared his father's passion for learning and literary ambitions but also to have assumed his

10 See Paul Walsh, 'Janet Marward, 1562–1629', *Irish Book Lover* 24 (1936), 99–104.

11 *New Oxford dictionary of national biography*, pp 272–3. For a further biographical account of William Nugent, see the entry on 'Uilliam Nuinseann' in Máire Ní Mhurchú and Diarmuid Breathnach (eds), *1560–1781 Beathasinéis* (Dublin, 2001), pp 97–8. *The green cockatrice* by Basil Iske, the pen-name of the Meath historian, Elisabeth Hickey, is a book-length biography of William Nugent. It attempts a continuous narrative of Nugent's life but is marred by many errors, despite its evident passion for its subject. Above all, its idiosyncratic claim that Nugent is either the addressee of Shakespeare's sonnets or even the author of them strains credulity.

erstwhile career as an insurgent. He was a supporter of the Gaelic chiefs during the campaigns of Hugh O'Neill. A letter, dated 31 March 1600, from a spy who was based at O'Neill's camp, addressed to the Secretary of the Privy Council, Sir Geoffrey Fenton, records the presence of William Nugent's son, Richard, along with his confederate, Thomas Shelton. In August 1600, another note written by a spy relates that Nugent and Shelton are en route to Scotland in the company of Walter Stanihurst. Thomas Shelton (fl.1598–1629) is a singular figure who sheds interesting light on Richard Nugent and affords us a purchase on his cultural and political allegiances. He suggests in particular a link between the Nugents and the transnational migrant Catholic communities of Counter-Reformation Europe, and the dissenting politics and urbane multiculturalism that they espoused. What is particularly germane about the friendship between the two men is the fact that it is sewn into the material fabric of *Cynthia,* as Shelton is one of the intimate associates who responds to the sequence and unreservedly applauds its artistry in a truncated eleven-line sonnet that forms part of the coda. Born in Dublin, Shelton came from an Old English family which was as known for its fractiousness as that of Nugent. His father, Henry Shelton, was a merchant who was imprisoned in 1596 for refusing to take the oath of supremacy.[12] Shelton may have been educated in the Irish college at Salamanca.[13] It is likely that it was here that he acquired the proficiency in Spanish which he drew upon both in his political involvements and his career as a writer. Shelton is above all known to posterity as the first translator into English of Miguel de Cervantes's *Don Quixote* which, with characteristic panache, he claims to have completed in the space of a few months as a gift to a companion who had requested it.[14] Moreover, it may well be that his hastily compiled translation is a

12 See Jonathan Lambe's account of Shelton in *New Oxford dictionary of national biography*, pp 221–5.

13 On the history of the involvement of Irish students in the College of Salamanca, see Thomas Morrissey, 'The Irish student diaspora in the sixteenth century and the early years of the Irish college at Salamanca', *Recusant History* 14 (1978), 242–60.

14 In the preface to *The history of the valorous and wittie knight-errant, Don-Quixote of the Mancha translated out of the Spanish. The first parte History of Don-Quichote* (London, 1612), Shelton explains to his patron Lord Howard de Walden that he had translated *Don Quixote* from Spanish in the 'space of fortie daies' (p. 2) some five or six years earlier in answer to the 'importunitie of a very deere friend' who was keen to learn about the text. Shelton based his translation not on the Spanish original but on an imprint in Spanish that appeared in Brussels in 1607. In 1620 he completed his translation of the second part of the text and published a revised edition of the first part, *The second part of the history of the valorous and witty knight-errant, Don Quixote of the Mancha. Written in Spanish by Michael Cervantes and now translated into English* (London, 1620). It it noteworthy that Shelton includes in the introductory matter and epilogue spoof sonnets supposedly penned by fictional characters such as Amadis of Gaul and Orlando Furioso and even by the characters of Cervantes's novel itself. Such playfulness is evidence of the sophisticated attitude to the production of sonnets in the literary circles in which Nugent moved.

further material link with the author of *Cynthia* since, as Knowles contends, there is a likelihood that it was expressly to satisfy the intellectual curiosity of Richard Nugent that he produced this text.[15] In late 1598, his oldest brother John was involved in an unsuccessful attempt to capture Dublin Castle for Hugh O'Neill. He was hanged and Thomas was sought by the authorities as an accomplice. Despite the constant danger of arrest and execution, it is likely that he remained in Ireland until 1601, as in that year he offered his services to Florence MacCarthy, the Irish rebel, in a letter written in Spanish that was intercepted by the authorities and added to the intelligence file on him. Nugent and Shelton may have travelled to Spain in 1601, later moving to the Spanish Netherlands. Knowles records that Nugent joined the Irish regiment there, a detail omitted from other accounts of his life.[16] After this, gaps appear once again in the records. It is known that Nugent died in or around this period but the circumstances of his death and the precise year are uncertain. An elegy 'In Memori Ricardi Nugent', composed in Irish supposedly in 1604 by his friend the bardic poet, Giolla Brighde Ó heoghusa (Bonaventura O'Hussey), supplies us with a final moving vignette.[17] The elegy is addressed to the poet's mother, Janet, and is included in the 'Book of O'Conor Don', compiled in Ostend in 1631. In the first half of the text, Ó heoghusa concentrates on the debilitating pain of the wound of grief and dwells especially on the unremitting sorrow experienced by his mother. The latter half of the poem counterbalances this devastating mood by shifting to an encomium of the deceased. In conventional manner, a ritualized but affecting list of the virtues and accomplishments of Nugent is compiled:

> Oighre Sgríne na sgoth nglas
> brath Dealbhna na ndionn solas
> glún uaislighthe an fhine ó bhfuil,
> cridhe an ghuaisbheithre i ngalaibh.
>
> Bláth ógán Innse na bhFionn,
> foithne Rois, Risdeard Nuinnsionn,
> draig roighreanta, beithir borb,
> feithimh móirshleachta Marbhord.

15 Knowles, p. 168.

16 Knowles, p. 167.

17 See Osborne Bergin, *Irish bardic poetry* (Dublin, 1984), pp 142–5. Giolla Brighde Ó heoghusa was born in Co. Fermanagh and educated at Douai and Leuven where he became a Franciscan priest and guardian of St Anthony's College. He was known for his wide knowledge of Irish language and literature and lectured at the University of Leuven in theology and philosophy. In 1611, he published, *An teagasg criosdaidhe*, the first printed catechism to use an Irish typeface. See Thomas Wall, 'Bonaventure O'Hussey', *Irish Ecclesiastical Record* 59 (1942), 36–48.

Saor an sgoth do sgar ruibhse,
ní hiongadh t'fháth doghuilse:
ba triall raith, ba gaoth in ngal,
ba laoch, ba flaith, ba feallsamh.

Níor chlannaigh fa choim na neamh
ní nach fuair fios a airrdhean,
re hais gcearcaill na cruinne,
ná a seantruim thais talmhaidhe.

[The heir of Skreen of the verdant shoots, the hope of Delvin of the bright hillocks, the generation that ennobled his race, the hero's heart in battle.

Flower of the youth of the Island of the Fair, shelter of Ros, Richard Nugent, handsome champion, fierce warrior, guardian of Marward's great line.

Noble was the young scion that has parted from thee, no marvel is thy reason for sorrow. His career was happy; he was wise in conflict, he was a fighter, a leader, a scholar.

He planted nothing under heaven's canopy whereof he learned not the attributes, besides the circle of the universe and its moist earthly centre.][18]

Ó heoghusa explicitly draws attention to Nugent's learning and prowess as a warrior. But the particulars of his career and especially his accomplishment as a writer are submerged in the moving rhetoric of the elegiac formulae of this bardic poem.

As the historian Fionnán Tuite has recently contended, the friendship with Thomas Shelton provides compelling evidence that Richard Nugent, son of William Nugent, may be identified as the author of *Cynthia*.[19] Historical sources specifically tie him to Shelton and not to Richard, son of Nicholas Nugent. However, this attribution remains merely a strong probability and is offered here as a further intervention in the still-unsettled debates surrounding the authorship

18 Translation by Osborne Bergin. See Bergin, p. 144 and pp 278–9.

19 This information has been supplied by Fionnán Tuite in personal correspondence with the editor, Angelina Lynch. Tuite has completed a doctorate entitled 'Politics in Meath 1534–1603' at the School of History and Archives, University College Dublin. See Fionnán Tuite, 'Familial feud in early modern Meath' in Robert Armstrong and Tadhg Ó hAnnracháin (eds), *Community in early modern Ireland* (Dublin, 2006), pp 69–90, for an examination of the Nugent-Dillon feud in the late sixteenth century.

of *Cynthia*. Moreover, although this identification renders some aspects of the sequence more readily explicable, particularly the addition of the final sonnet in Italian reporting on the unexpected and premature death of the author, it leaves many questions unanswered. It is unclear, for example, whether Nugent had time to bring his work to completion, albeit as later discussion will show, the sequence is carefully crafted and ordered and does not exhibit signs of hasty assemblage. Above all, the identity of the author of the final Italian sonnet is unknown and the circumstances surrounding the publication of the text are seemingly lost to us. It seems probable that friends or relatives of Nugent ensured the publication of the volume in London in 1604 as a posthumous tribute. Perhaps William Nugent, his father – who was himself an accomplished poet in both Irish and English – played a role in compiling the volume. He may also have appended the final text, as it is likely that he had some proficiency in Italian. But it can likewise be mooted that Thomas Shelton, a multilingual poet and translator, could just as easily have fulfilled these roles.

Further tantalizing questions must also be flagged in relation to the publication history of *Cynthia*. The choice of publisher seems to have been apposite, as Thomas Purfoot (fl.1566), a freeman of the Stationers' Company, printed an eclectic list of literary works by Francis Bacon, George Fletcher, William Shakespeare and Thomas Heywood amongst others.[20] He also produced work as an assign to George Tottel and hence was associated with the dissemination of the popular *Tottel's miscellany*, a volume which was responsible for introducing the sonnet form to an English public for the first time and triggering the vogue for this mode of composition. His production of *Cynthia* is hence unexceptional and is in consonance with his profile and commercial concerns as a publisher. However, on another level, the text appears to be an anomaly, as Purfoot did not publish any other book with an Irish provenance. Even though it is overtly secular in tenor, *Cynthia*, the product ultimately of a nascent but self-conscious Catholic Counter-Reformation milieu, sits oddly in the overall output of Purfoot who also specialized in Protestant polemic and devotional literature and anti-Catholic invective.[21] Several feasible explanations that account for Purfoot's readiness to print this text may be proffered: it could be that its potentially seditious features are so expertly concealed and camouflaged that they did not draw attention to themselves or that the publication of a compact volume of poetry was simply a matter of commercial expediency that overrode any problematic taint that might have stigmatized the text.

20 For a brief account of Purfoot, see E. Gordon Duff, *A century of the English book trade* (London, 1905).

21 Purfoot, moreover, frequently functioned as a 'searcher' for the Stationers' Company seeking out unlawful publications that infringed the privileges of the organization.

However, as with many other aspects of *Cynthia*, questions still linger that cannot satisfactorily be answered as to how its publication was engineered and who oversaw and facilitated the process. Additionally, its readership cannot reliably be ascertained, even though it seems likely that it was destined in the first instance to be read *in memoriam* by the close friends of the poet. But as these were scattered throughout England, Ireland and Europe, this was in itself a potentially diverse and international audience. Additionally, *Cynthia* would also have enjoyed a certain cachet and marketability due to the still current fashion for sonnet sequences which had reached its pinnacle in the late 1590s but had by no means fully ebbed. Ambiguously, then, the volume would seem to target the intersecting interests of a discerning coterie readership and the tastes of a broader literary public. The fact that the text was not reissued is not unusual. As Marcy L. North points out, most sonnet sequences were written for publication but few underwent a second printing.[22]

In sum, the precise details of the biography of Richard Nugent and the circumstances culminating in the printing of his text remain obdurately obscured due to what appear to be irretrievable gaps in the historical records. Currently available evidence has led to divergent but always necessarily provisional conclusions about the figure of the author. It is likely that future research by historians may render the attribution of *Cynthia* more secure. However, although such verification will be welcome, it must also be underlined that sonnet sequences can never merely be seen as veiled biographies. The personal history of the author, as a consequence, provides only one of the several material dimensions by which such texts may be scrutinized and interpreted. The historical realities that they encode are oblique and imbricated in complex social and political contexts that need to be carefully unearthed. As John Kerrigan has argued in relation to the biographical debates that surround Shakespeare's sonnets, the poet certainly stands behind the first person of his poems but he also exists at some remove from the literary personae that he creates.[23] A similar claim may be put forward with respect to Richard Nugent who is both the subject of, and hidden behind, the poetic fiction that he invents. What is of moment in *Cynthia* is not only its delineation of a subjective history – the factual dimensions of which will always be indeterminate – but also its pointed evocation of the cultural and political environment of an Old English sept in late sixteenth-century Ireland and of the geopolitics of a borderland community subsisting within and on the verge of the Pale.

22 Marcy L. North, 'The sonnets and book history', p. 209.

23 John Kerrigan, 'Introduction', William Shakespeare, *The Sonnets and A Lover's Complaint* (London, 1986), p. 11.

II: THE OLD ENGLISH AND PROBLEMS OF ALLEGIANCE

The particularity of Nugent's sonnet sequence may be sought less in the contours of his own private fate than in the wider ambit of his family history and the particular social class to which he belonged, namely the Old English. The varying designations given to the latter, including the Anglo-Normans, the Anglo-Irish, *Anglo-Hiberni*, and (in Irish) the *sean-Ghaill*, are themselves indicative of the contradictory positions of this hybrid settler class and of the difficulties they increasingly encountered in defining their social and political roles in the late sixteenth and seventeenth centuries.[24] Descendants of the twelfth-century invaders, who were of diverse ethnic origins, the Old English over time intermarried with the local population and adopted Irish customs and language. However, simultaneously, they retained a loyalty to the Crown and continued to support and affiliate themselves with English culture. The assimilation to Irish ways of this social grouping as well as its flexible bi-culturalism as it moved readily between Gaelic and Anglophone spheres opened it to the suspicion of the so-called New English who became mouthpieces of an aggressively reformulated colonizing ideology and promulgators of the renewed drive for conquest and plantation of the Elizabethan regime. Further adding to the difference of the Old English was their Catholicism and loyalty to Rome, as the English administrators, governors and soldiers who drove the revivified Tudor urge to conquer and reform the country were Protestant in persuasion.

The latter half of the sixteenth century marks the period in which notions of the Old English emerged and evolved. As Nicholas Canny notes, the term did not exist at the accession of Elizabeth I in 1553, but had achieved currency by the beginning of the seventeenth century.[25] In effect, the changes in policy of the Elizabethan regime put pressure on these long-standing colonists who had acculturated to Irish ways to assert their inherited rights as landowners and rulers, ensure their continuing ownership of their dominions and properties, attest to their pluralist sense of heritage, learning and status and proclaim their continued if increasingly conflicted loyalty to the Crown. Moreover, their various efforts to give voice to and articulate their sense of their identity in this period must also be seen as counter-ideological, as they are at pains to refute the prejudicial views being formulated by New English writers such as Edmund Spenser, who in *A*

24 The term *Anglo-Hiberni*, which translates literally as the English-Irish, is a coinage of Richard Stanihurst and deployed by him in *De rebus in Hibernia gestis libri quattuor* (Antwerp, 1584). For an analysis of the political nuances of the shifting nomenclature used by Stanihurst in his descriptions of Ireland and defence of English culture in the country, see Colm Lennon, *The life of Richard Stanihurst the Dubliner, 1547–1618* (Dublin, 1981), pp 79–83.

25 Nicholas Canny, *The formation of the Old English elite in Ireland* (Dublin, 1974), pp 2–39 (p. 2).

view of the state of Ireland unreservedly castigates their degeneracy and lack of moral and political integrity.[26] In addition, it is important to recognize that the notion of a circumscribed Old English culture that is being proposed here is neither a conceptual monolith nor an expression of an unchanging *mentalité* but rather an area of contestation and of ongoing and shifting renegotiation.[27]

In his ground-breaking study, Aidan Clarke argues that the Old English felt themselves to be increasingly under siege and alienated throughout the initial decades of the seventeenth century and that, as a result, they eventually abandoned their time-honoured weapons of compromise and moderation by joining the Irish in rebellion in 1641.[28] Clarke's study of the Old English takes 1625 as its point of departure. The history of the Nugent family in the later decades of the sixteenth century indicates that his theses also have validity for this earlier era. Moreover, it is evident that many other breaking points leading to rebellion occur prior to 1641. Hence, it may be more apt to see the Old English as alternatively torn between rebellion and compromise from the Tudor period onwards. Furthermore, it became increasingly difficult for this beset community to negotiate the divisions between treason and loyalty. This is especially clear in the case of the Nugents who were caught up in the closing decades of the sixteenth century in local rivalries that spilled over into the upheavals caused by the redistribution of power and favour effected by the new colonial regime and in the violent repressiveness of opposition that it favoured. Further, many of the key members of the family made frequent shifts from loyal to rebellious subject or from insurgency to quiescence depending on political exigency. In the conflicted relations with state authority of the Nugent family, fealty was always in flux and subject to the demands of *realpolitik*. Such instability, as will later be argued, may be seen to inform the emotional dynamics of *Cynthia,* as it explores the volatile relationship between the poet and his beloved and its ever-changing balance of power.

The rebellion led by William Nugent in 1580–1 represented a particular turning point in the fortunes of the family and also crystallized the degree to which the central administration was intent on curtailing the traditional entitlements of the Old English lords and saw them as a threat to the state. Helen

26 On the vices of the Old English who 'are degenerated and grown almost mere Irish', see Andrew Hadfield and Willy Maley (eds), Edmund Spenser, *A view of the state of Ireland* (Oxford, 1997), p. 54.

27 On the necessity for viewing the different ethnic identities and *mentalités* in Renaissance Ireland as ambiguous and multi-faceted, see Vincent P. Carey and Ute Lotz-Heumann (eds), 'Introduction' to *Taking sides?: colonial and confessional* mentalités *in early modern Ireland* (Dublin, 2003), pp 1–18.

28 Aidan Clarke, *The Old English in Ireland, 1625–42* (1966; repr. Dublin, 2000).

Coburn Walshe in her detailed assessment of this rebellion argues that, while it retrenched the power of the gentry in the Pale, it did not necessarily drive them wholly to embrace the values of the Counter-Reformation.[29] She recognizes, however, that the insurgency of William Nugent was fundamentally political in nature even though he did not overtly invoke Catholic ideals and values. It was motivated not just by local grievances or self-interest but by the increasing recognition that the communal identity of the Old English was under pressure in the emerging colonial order. S.J. Connolly makes a similar case and argues that the growing intransigence of the new regime on matters of religion forced the Old English to recalculate their political position by assuming facets of Counter-Reformation thinking and also by tapping into their alliances in Gaelic Ireland.[30] The execution of Nicholas Nugent for treason was brought about by the machinations of Sir Robert Dillon who felt that he had wrongly been granted the office of chief justice of the common pleas which he had sought for himself. It may thus be seen as the result of a long-standing inter-familial feud and a matter merely of local politics. But the circumstances of William Nugent's rebellion made it possible for Dillon's vendetta to manipulate the regime and ensure the dispatch of his rival as intimate rivalries fed into large-scale patterns of confessional change and ideological shifts in power. Hence, in the Nugent rebellion, a local enmity was translated into a broader arena that pitted the colonizing zeal of the Protestant New English against the Catholic Old English who faced dispossession. The latter found themselves torn between political groupings: they pursued commonalities with Gaelic Ireland while stoutly defending the representative rights once accorded to them by English constitutionality and aligning themselves haphazardly with the different constituencies of Counter-Reformation Europe.

The fact that three of the principal immediate male forbears of Richard Nugent – Nicholas Nugent, William Nugent and Christopher Nugent – were all at different stages of their lives accused of treason, imprisoned and faced with the ultimate sanction of execution is indicative of the upheavals within his family and the degree to which clashes with the state materially impinged on his everyday existence. Moreover, the lives of the Nugents were bound by ties of blood that were irredeemably political and not merely tribal. During the rebellion of 1581, Richard, the son of Nicholas Nugent, was offered, for example, in surety to Dublin Castle for his cousin, Christopher, son of William Nugent. As has been illustrated, Nicholas Nugent seems to have been an unfortunate victim of

29 Helen Coburn Walshe, 'The rebellion of William Nugent, 1581' in R.V. Comerford, Mary Cullen, Jacqueline R. Hill and Colm Lennon (eds), *Religion, conflict and coexistence in Ireland: essays presented to Monsignor Patrick J. Corish* (Dublin, 1990), pp 26–52.

30 S.J. Connolly, *Contested island: Ireland 1460–1630* (Oxford, 2007), pp 200–14.

familial political intrigues that were beyond his control, but in which he was inextricably entangled. By contrast, William Nugent despite his rebelliousness as a young man would appear to have made an accommodation with the system after his pardon and retired to a peaceful existence on his estates at the end of his days. Yet, a bitterness about the unjust execution of his uncle Nicholas and a quest for retribution occupied much of the latter part of his existence.

The life of his brother, Christopher Nugent (1544–1602), fifth Baron Delvin, follows a far more tragic course.[31] His career was particularly bedevilled by the torn allegiances he inherited from his background and upbringing. Delvin was active in the service of the English regime in Ireland. He fought in the campaigns against Shane O'Neill and was proud of his English heritage. Bilingual like all of the members of his family, he was, as a consequence, a strong and outspoken advocate of Irish culture. He continued to act as patron of the bardic clan of the Ó Cobhthaigh, based at Uisneach in Co. Westmeath, who had traditionally been allies of the Nugents and composed for them. In 1562, while a student in Cambridge he had prepared an Irish primer for Queen Elizabeth I. It consisted of an Irish alphabet, a glossary in Irish, Latin and English and a short history of the Irish language. In the preface he appeals to the queen's 'desyer ... to understand the language of your people' and thus depicts Irish not as barbarous tongue but as an inherent part of the transnational and pluralist culture of England and Ireland.[32] But he also recommends Irish as an instrument of reform and a means of fully ensuring the obedience of a recalcitrant colony. Delvin, despite his proclaimed loyalty, was under suspicion by the regime, due to his recusancy and his entangled relations with Gaelic Ireland that had been forged through the marriage alliances of several of his children. He was placed under restraint in 1575 when he refused to sign a proclamation of rebellion against the earl of Desmond, and he was imprisoned in Dublin Castle in 1577 when he and several other Old English lords questioned the constitutionality of the imposition of cess. In the 1580s, he was implicated in the Baltinglass rebellion, captured and banished to England. He returned to Ireland in 1585 and, after much wrangling, re-established ownership of his estates. During the Nine Years War, he was suspected of partisanship with Hugh O'Neill and was arrested on these grounds in 1602 and held captive in Dublin Castle. He died there before a trial for treason against him could be mounted. As Colm Lennon observes, Delvin

31 For a discerning and layered account of Delvin's life, see Colm Lennon, *New Oxford dictionary of national biography*, pp 251–3.

32 John Thomas Gilbert (ed.), *Facsimiles of the National Manuscripts of Ireland* (London, 1882), vol. IV, 1, p. xxxv. For a discussion of Nugent's text and its underlying attitudes towards the Irish language, see Patricia Palmer, *Language and conquest in early modern Ireland: English Renaissance literature and Elizabethan imperial expansion* (Cambridge, 2001), pp 80–1.

was ultimately treated as culpable by virtue solely of his lineage and the inter-ethnic links of his family.[33] Tragically, he became a traitor by default. His membership of the ambiguous social and political worlds of the Old English community doomed him to inveterate opposition to a polity that he in fact attempted to defend.

Recent research has increasingly uncovered the degree to which the Old English sought to use print in order to give expression to their identity and values and to counter negative estimations of their ethos and traditions. Also, in the writing they produced or commissioned they attempted to give an account of their understanding of the overlapping but distinctive cultural contexts that defined them.[34] Thus, Richard Stanihurst in his supplement to Holinshed's history of Ireland goes to great lengths to produce an amenable portrait of the learning and achievements of the Old English and to edit out any allusions to their proficiency in Irish or knowledge of Gaelic culture.[35] The Nugents, contrary to Stanihurst's deliberately doctored view of things, pursue expression in both the Irish and the English cultural spheres and regularly override any lines of demarcation that might obtain between them. Indeed, the bardic poetry with which they were associated indicates that the family for decades had been a part of a hybridized social world in which cultural interaction counterbalanced, or even partly outweighed, political differences. An elegy written to mark the death of Richard Nugent, eighth baron of Delvin (d. 1559), 'Brónach Goill Bhanbha dá éis' ('Lonely are the Galls of Banba after him') depicts him firmly as an Englishman and a protector of the Pale, and situates him within the Old English community.[36] But the poem also lauds him for his patronage of Irish poets and

33 *New Oxford dictionary of national biography*, p. 253.

34 For a discussion of the importance of writing in the vernacular for the construction of ethnic and communal identities, see Adrian Hastings, *The construction of nationhood: ethnicity, religion and nationalism* (Cambridge, 1997), pp 1–34.

35 For an analysis of Stanihurst's remoulding of the second edition of Holinshed's text, see Richard A. McCabe, 'Making history: Holinshed's Irish *Chronicles*' in David J. Baker and Willy Maley (eds), *British identities and English Renaissance literature* (Cambridge, 2002), pp 51–67. Stanihurst, however, later revises this seeming denigration of the Irish language and learning after he leaves Ireland in 1581 for the Spanish Netherlands and begins to live openly as a Catholic exile and supporter of Hugh O'Neill. See Colm Lennon, *Richard Stanihurst, the Dubliner, 1547–1618*, pp 45–67 and pp 99–105 and Vincent Carey, 'A "dubious loyalty": Richard Stanihurst, the "wizard" earl of Kildare, and English-Irish identity' in Carey and Lotz-Heumann (eds), *Taking sides?: colonial and confessional* mentalités *in early modern Ireland*, pp 61–77.

36 Éamonn O Tuathail, 'Nugentiana', *Éigse* 2 (1940), 4–14 (pp 8–11). For a discussion of the import of this poem and a incisive rereading of the hybrid culture of the New English, see Vincent Carey, '"Neither good English nor good Irish": bi-lingualism and identity formation in sixteenth-century Ireland' in Hiram Morgan (ed.), *Political ideology in Ireland, 1541–1641* (Dublin, 1999), pp 45–61 (pp 53–4).

musicians and correlates him hence with 'Banba' and an Irish cultural milieu. Revealingly, the dual perspectives in this text are offered ultimately as complementary and are not viewed either as warring or at variance.

The bardic poems written by William Nugent provide further evidence of how the interaction between Irish and English cultures on the borderlands of the Pale produced affinities and alliances that are capable of overwriting, or at least mediating, political difference. But, equally, as Marc Caball has persuasively contended, his texts illustrate the degree to which Old English identity now defines itself in contradistinction to projected notions of England and Englishness.[37] Nugent, who as Mícheál Mac Craith notes was one of the first bardic poets to reflect on the theme of exile and to turn it to political account, supposedly wrote one of his poems on this topic, 'Diombáidh triall ó thulchaibh Fáil' ('It is sorrowful to leave the hills of Ireland'), when he left for Oxford in 1571.[38] In it, he paints a picture of Ireland as a *locus amoenus*, an impossibly idyllic location peopled by poets, warriors and golden-haired women. His home-sickness for Banba is so great, he tells us, that if he had the chance to return he would never again desire to visit the noble families of England. In this poetic evocation of the plight of the emigrant, England is emphatically described as a place of lack by comparison with the social and cultural richness of his native country. Ireland is self-consciously evoked as a totality and deployed strategically as a trope of plenitude. In another of Nugent's poems of exile, 'Fada i n-éagmais inse Fáil' ('In England, far away from Ireland'), his feelings of dislocation in England, where time passes more slowly than in Ireland, are used as a basis for circumscribing his love for his home-place and for his fellow countrymen.[39] What is striking about this text is that it envisages Nugent's country people in unitary terms. As a collective they encompass both 'Gaill' and 'Gaoidhil'. Even though Irishness and Englishness are at odds outside of the country, within it they are, at least momentarily through the alchemy of poetic vision, confederated and aligned:

37 Marc Caball, 'Faith, culture and sovereignty: Irish nationalism and its development, 1558–1625' in Brendan Bradshaw and Peter Roberts (eds), *British consciousness and identity: the making of Britain, 1533–1709* (Cambridge, 1998), pp 112–39 (p. 118).

38 Gerard Murphy, 'Poems of Exile by Uilliam Nuinseann Mac Barúin Dealbhna', *Éigse* 6 (1945–52), 8–15 (pp 11–13). For an earlier analysis and translation of this poem which however assumes that the poem is written by an unknown bard about the enforced exile of a son of Christopher Nugent, see Paul Walsh, 'Farewell to Innisfail', *Gleanings from Irish manuscripts* (Dublin, 1933), pp 3–11. On Nugent as a poet of exile and his depiction of a Gaelic Catholic patrimony jointly owned by the native Irish and the Old English alike, see Mícheál Mac Craith, 'Literature in Irish, *c.*1550–1690' in Margaret Kelleher and Philip O' Leary (eds), *The Cambridge history of Irish literature volume I: to 1890* (Cambridge, 2006), pp 191–231 (p. 219).

39 Murphy, 'Poems of Exile by Uilliam Nuinseann Mac Barúin Dealbhna', pp 13–15.

A haifrinn, a huird chrábhaidh,
A haos ciúil (mo chompánuigh),
filidh cláir Ghall a's Ghaoidheal.
Ann is cáir do chommaoidheamh.

[Her masses, her religious orders, her musicians who were my companions, and the poets of that land where Gaill (Anglo-Normans) and Gaoidhil (Irish) dwell: all should be included in our enumeration.][40]

It would appear that Nugent's projection of Ireland as a territorial whole allows him to forge a vision of an inclusive ethnicity.[41] The act of imagining his homeland from the alienated viewpoint of the exile permits not only a vision of harmonious encompassment but also the articulation of a precise sense of national difference.

The multiple but intersecting cultural and political worlds of the Old English have been variously defined and explicated. Marc Caball holds that the ethnic coalescence of families such as the Nugents with native Gaelic traditions facilitated the emergence of an Irish cultural patriotism.[42] Vincent Carey contends that the historic rapprochement between Gaelic and Old English communities on the borderlands of the Pale produced a hybridized dynastic culture and forged new modes of political identity that can properly be examined only in comparative frameworks.[43] Clare Carroll likewise deems it necessary to view the writing of early modern Ireland not merely in the 'three kingdoms' context advocated by the New British history but also in terms of the literature of Catholic Europe.[44] John Kerrigan, by contrast, argues for an enlarged and complicated interpretation of Englishness which has erroneously been seen as a fixed entity in the early modern period. Instead of functioning as a monolith, for Kerrigan, it is characterized by a devolutionary and interactive dynamics and, as a consequence, the identity of groups such as the Old English is simultaneously local, Continental and archipelagic.[45] Nugent's *Cynthia* bears out these assessments of the complex political positioning of the Old English community and of the new cultural imaginary which it was beginning to forge in the late sixteenth century. It evinces a keen awareness of the problematics of identity and political allegiance and sheds important light on how an Old English poet

40 Murphy, 'Poems of Exile by Uilliam Nuinseann Mac Barúin Dealbhna', p. 15.

41 This important point is made by Caball. See 'Faith, culture and sovereignty', p. 118.

42 Marc Caball, *Poets and politics: reaction and continuity in Irish poetry, 1558–1625* (Cork, 1998).

43 Carey, 'Bi-lingualism and identity formation in sixteenth-century Ireland', pp 60–1.

44 Clare Carroll, *Circe's cup: cultural transformations in early modern Ireland* (Cork, 2001), pp 1–10.

45 John Kerrigan, *Archipelagic English: literature, history, and politics 1603–1707* (Oxford, 2008), pp 1–90.

reshapes anglophone writing to voice his sense of hybridity, attachment and dislocation. It at once seeks to elaborate the co-ordinates of Irish national belonging and to come to grips with the volatile entities of English allegiance and royalist devotion. The unique emphasis on locality and the peculiar concentration on the themes of fealty and betrayal in this sonnet sequence, it will emerge, are inherently bound up with the contested and fragile political environment in which the author lived and the multi-ethnic social worlds to which he belonged. Indeed, it will be argued that *Cynthia* attempts to achieve a reconciliation on a symbolic plane of political differences which in reality were proving increasingly problematic and divisive.

III: THE EARLY MODERN SONNET SEQUENCE

The sonnet is a belated arrival in England. It was created by Giacomo da Lentino (b. ?1210) who was a notary and official at the court of the Hohenstaufen Holy Roman Emperor Frederick II, who ruled over the Kingdom of the Two Sicilies from 1208 to 1250. Frederick was an enlightened but ruthless despot, and the form that da Lentino invented seems to have been aimed at other courtiers and to have masked its political content. As Paul Oppenheimer asserts, it was not only the first lyric mode intended for silent reading but also the first designed for the expression of inwardness and the portrayal of the self in conflict.[46] It was quickly taken up the poets of the *dolce stil nuovo*, most prominently Dante (*c*.1265–1321) in *La Vita Nuova* and Francesco Petrarca (1304–74) in *Canzoniere*. It entered Spanish literature in the mid-fifteenth century and became part of the vernaculars of Britain and France in the early sixteenth century. The work of the first practitioners of the sonnet in England, Sir Thomas Wyatt (?1503–42) and Henry Howard, earl of Surrey (?1517–47), was published posthumously in 1557 in a volume that has become known as *Tottel's miscellany*.[47] While this collection popularized the form and – even more importantly – introduced the public to Wyatt's innovative restructuring of the final lines as a couplet, it may also have retarded the development of the English sonnet sequence, as Michael Spiller points out, due to its jumbled presentation, concentration on the discrete poem as opposed to the collection and its interspersing of sonnets with other short lyrics.[48] However, its influence is undoubted and, after its publication, writers of

46 Paul Oppenheimer, *The birth of the modern mind: self, consciousness, and the invention of the sonnet* (Oxford, 1989), pp 3–40.

47 Its original title is *Songes and sonettes written by the ryght honorable lorde Henry Haward late earle of Surrey, and other*.

48 Michael R.G. Spiller, *The development of the sonnet: an introduction* (London, 1992), pp 92–5.

sonnets in English adhere to the rhyme schemes initiated by Wyatt and Surrey and the culminating couplet that they had both developed.

The earliest critical commentaries on the sonnet in English allow us to pinpoint some of its chief properties, to reflect on its pliancy and to investigate the role of Petrarchism in defining its rhetorical structures, arguments and characteristic tropes. The sonnet is a so-called prescribed or closed form with a predetermined length of fourteen lines. George Gascoigne was the first to define the English sonnet in this manner, noting also that each line should contain ten syllables and that 'the first twelve do ryme in staves of foure lines by cross meetre, and the last two ryming togither do conclude the whole'.[49] The sonnet hence is prized because of its ability to shape experience and to transform the disorder of passion into an elegantly moulded artefact. Samuel Daniel lauds it precisely on these grounds and observes that the 'tyrannicall bounding of the conceit' in the sonnet, is not a hindrance. Rather, it allows the poet to transform the 'unformed *Chaos*' of the imagination into 'an Orbe of order and forme'.[50] Other commentaries, however, pick up on the opposing propensity of sonnets to favour excess and contrivance. Sir John Harrington, even while defending this form, observes that it often lapses into 'plaine scurrilitie', while Sir Philip Sidney declares that the amorous discourse of many sonneteers strikes him as artificial and studied and that if he 'were a mistress [it] would never persuade me that they were in love'.[51]

Formally, the sonnet also poses many challenges for the poet. The uneasy counterweighting of chaos and order and sincerity and affectation noted by early commentators is replicated by the potential asymmetry of its structure. In its Continental and English variants, the internal divisions of this poetic form serve both as a unifying armature and as a possible source of imbalance. In the Petrarchan sonnet, the fourteen lines are divided into two disproportionate halves. However, the *volta* or turn in the argument at the end of the octave provides the means of knitting it with the sestet. In the so-called Shakespearean sonnet, which had in fact been invented by Wyatt and Surrey, the integration of the three quatrains and the couplet is effected by the interweave of the argument and the cross-rhymes and by the clarifying effect of the epigrammatic insight

49 George Gascoigne, *Certayne notes of instruction concerning the making of verse or ryme in English, written at the request of Master Edouardo Donati* (1575) in G. Gregory Smith (ed.), *Elizabethan critical essays*. 2 vols (Oxford, 1904), I, pp 46–57 (p. 55).

50 Samuel Daniel, *A defence of ryme: against a pamphlet entitled: observations in the art of English poesie. Wherein is demonstratively proved, that ryme is fittest harmonie of words that comportes with our language* (1603; London, 1950), pp 127–58 (p. 138).

51 Sir John Harrington, *A brief apology for poetry* (1591) in G. Gregory Smith (ed.), *Elizabethan critical essays*, II, pp 194–222 (p. 209). Sir Philip Sidney, *The defence of poesy* (1595) in Katherine Duncan-Jones (ed.), *Sir Philip Sidney: the major works* (1989; Oxford, 2002), pp 212–50 (p. 246).

provided at the poem's close. In view of this complex architectonics, the chief objectives of the poet are, as Michael R.G. Spiller contends, 'coming to the point' and ensuring the cohesion of a form that is as predicated on disarray as the skilful intermarriage of its component parts.[52]

Petrarch's love sonnets act as a germinal influence on all subsequent writing in this tradition. The *Rime sparse* (*Scattered rhymes*) or *Canzoniere* is a carefully fashioned two-part sequence which incorporates several different poetic forms and treats of the vicissitudes of the author's unrequited but enduring desire for Laura. It is not simply the latter's rejection of the poet that fuels his mediations but also her protean nature. While Laura is depicted as a quintessence of physical beauty or the target of erotic desire, she is also envisaged as an image of virtue and heavenly love and as an alter ego of the poet, channelling his creativity and linguistic prowess. She is on the one hand a cynosure and an inspiring visionary ideal and on the other an inimical force whose sadism induces pain and suffering and even visits death on her admirer. Further complicating the sequence is the fact that over half-way through – in poem 267 – Laura passes away and hence the collection divides, as commentators have pointed out, into lyrics written *in vivo* and *in morte*, to a beloved living and dead.[53] The poet moreover veers between idolatry and religious conversion while endeavouring to trace his moral growth and passage from youthful profligacy and uncontrolled passion to the wisdom of renunciation and sublimated desire. The final canzone addressed to the Virgin 'clothed in the sun's light' lastingly transposes the image of Laura from an earthly to a heavenly dimension and shifts the poet's love to a spiritual plane.[54]

Petrarchism is above all a discourse of extremes which depends upon the manipulation of oxymora, hyperbole and elaborate conceits of warfare and feudal devotion.[55] The lover fights against the constraints of desire and longs to be free of them, but is ultimately incapable of renouncing his feelings. Hence, the paradoxical metaphors of Petrarchan poetry draw out the ambiguity of his situation and the conflicted and self-undermining nature of his emotions. The woman is a sweet enemy whose iciness contrasts with the firiness of her suitor's passion. Love is conceived of as life and death simultaneously, while devotion to

52 Spiller, *The development of the sonnet*, p. 11.

53 For a discussion of the figure of Laura, see Mark Musa with Barbara Manfredi, 'Introduction', Petrarch, *The canzoniere or rerum vulgarium fragmenta*, translated into verse with notes and commentary by Mark Musa (Bloomington, 1996), pp xi–xxxiv.

54 Petrarch, *The canzoniere*, pp 510–17 (p. 511).

55 On the poetics of Petrarchism, see Leonard Forster, *The icy fire: five studies in european Petrarchism* (Cambridge, 1969) and Lisle Cecil John, *The Elizabethan sonnet sequences: studies in conventional conceits* (New York, 1964).

the beloved is the expression of ardent desire, a means of self-empowerment and an abject abasement to a hostile authority. Even though the woman is projected as a heavenly ideal and an impossibly remote abstraction, she is also viewed as an object of carnal love whose body parts in stylized manner can be catalogued and fetishized.

The extravagant poetics and psychological impasses of Petrarchism readily lent themselves to parody. However, as Heather Dubrow argues, Petrarchism and counter-Petrarchism cannot be conveniently separated into two distinct modes.[56] Rather, they shade into one another. Critique and self-reflection are as much part of the Petrarchan tradition as of those texts that set out to attack it.[57] The uneasy relationship between success and failure in Renaissance sonnets and their constant oscillation between moments of triumph and defeat allow the poet to inspect the values of competing status systems and to review the ways in which varying ideologies conflict. Unresolved conflict may be the perdurable scenario envisaged by such love poetry, but the iteration of stock images does not preclude scrutiny of the operations of power and of the double binds of attachment in which the author finds himself implicated.

IV: 'CYNTHIA': THE POETICS OF INTERTEXTUALITY

Cynthia has thus far garnered little attention from literary critics. It is itemized but not commented on by Thomas Roche in his magisterial study of the structures and numerological patterns of the Renaissance sonnet.[58] Marcy L. North cites Nugent's *Cynthia* in passing as an example of a multi-sequence publication that indicates the gradual composition of groups of sonnets over a period of time.[59] Tony Sweeney, in listing it in his catalogue of early Irish books, creates the first inventory that groups Nugent's work with other significant texts produced in Ireland.[60] Gerald Power in his detailed historical analysis of the text speculates about its literary qualities and comes to the conclusion that it exhibits the cultural conflictedness of the Old English. Even though the author is disaffected with the state and adheres to a form of emerging Irish patriotism, he yet

56 Heather Dubrow, *Echoes of desire: English Petrarchism and its counterdiscourses* (Ithaca, 1995).

57 On the fragmented subjectivity that underlies Petrarch's verse, see Giuseppe Mazzotta, 'The "Canzoniere" and the language of the self', *Studies in Philology* 75 (1978), 271–96.

58 Thomas P. Roche, *Petrarch and the English sonnet sequences* (New York, 1989), p. 520.

59 Marcy L. North, 'The sonnets and book history', p. 215.

60 Tony Sweeney, *Ireland and the printed word: a short descriptive catalogue of early books* (Dublin, 1997), p. 529. Sweeney notes that Nugent has the distinction of being the first Irish-born writer of published English verse.

resorts to a metropolitan English mode when it comes to seeking an artistic vehicle for his ideas and feelings.[61] Thomas Herron in an instructive unpublished paper has examined the Catholic subtexts of Nugent's poem and probed its use of Marian imagery.[62] Apart from these commentaries, *Cynthia*, however, has been by and large overlooked as a variant in a minor key of the early modern sonnet in English.

The first scholar to draw attention at length to this text and to rescue it from silence is Andrew Carpenter in his pioneering anthology of poetry from Renaissance Ireland.[63] Carpenter's excerpts underscore the sophistication of Nugent's artistry and pick out those sonnets that explicitly highlight place – as in the allusion in I.xi to 'this sweete isle' – and the theme of exile. In addition, the anthology as a whole invites a re-contextualization of *Cynthia* within a continuous history of anglophone writing in Ireland that is diverse, transnational and, in John Kerrigan's phrase, archipelagic. However, in demonstrating the extent to which Nugent endeavours to lend peculiarly Irish inflections to the sonnet, Carpenter also alerts us to indigenous strains within this overarching tradition which warrant additional explication. His framing of the selections from *Cynthia* hence provides suggestive directions for further investigation which the interpretation offered in this and the following section proposes to follow.[64]

Even though *Cynthia,* as later discussion will show, is at pains to replicate many of the stock images and motifs of the Renaissance sonnet, it also subverts and adds to inherited practices in telling ways. Sonnets, as Edward Hirsch and Eavan Boland have observed, particularly 'reverberate with the memory of other sonnets', but the form also appeals because of its pliability and nomadic nature.[65] Here, I shall first list the individual features of Nugent's composition which make it stand out from comparable texts in the period before proceeding to an analysis of its main tropes and intertexts.[66] Even in its seeming conventionalism, as will become apparent, *Cynthia* regularly departs from standard meaning. For

61 Gerald Power, 'An expression of Old English identity', p. 79.

62 'Richard Nugent's *Cynthia* (1604): Dreams of a "Hevenley Queen"', Conference of the Society of Renaissance Studies, 10 July 2008, Trinity College Dublin.

63 Andrew Carpenter (ed.), *Verse in English from Tudor and Stuart Ireland* (Cork, 2003), pp 125–7.

64 This analysis also extends and revises a previous investigation of *Cynthia*, See Anne Fogarty, 'Literature in English, 1550–1690' in Kelleher and Philip O' Leary (eds), *The Cambridge history of Irish literature volume I: to 1890*, pp 140–90 (p. 156).

65 Edward Hirsch and Eavan Boland, *The making of a sonnet: a Norton anthology* (New York, 2008), p. 54.

66 My reading of *Cynthia* is informed by William J. Kennedy's account of the way in which Petrarchism is redefined in different European contexts and made the vehicle for burgeoning nationalist discourses. See *The site of petrarchism: early modern national sentiment in Italy, France, and England* (Baltimore, 2003).

example, it uses the themes of temporality and mutability customarily highlighted by Renaissance sonnet sequences to give expression to a pervasive sense of devastating historical change and to articulate feelings of dispossession. By deploying the traditional bipartite structure of sonnet volumes, Nugent produces a remarkably cohesive sequence which also shows a decided shift in mood and darkening of tone in the second section. Contrary to decorum, however, *Cynthia* heightens the sense of grievance against the beloved generally voiced by the poet-lover and augments it so that disconcertingly, in Part Two of the sequence, it turns into a momentary quest for revenge.

Unlike many other poets, Nugent on occasion particularizes the universal metaphorical landscapes of the sonnet and obliquely but purposefully draws our attention to the transposition of this genre to the island of Ireland and to the Co. Westmeath lake-land terrain with which he would have been familiar. Further, the curious emphasis in several poems on the image of soil allows an implicit commentary on issues of supplantation and of proprietorship which exercised members of the Old English community in the late sixteenth century. Moreover, through exploiting the weight given to metacommentary and intertextuality in Renaissance sonnets, Nugent insinuates into *Cynthia* a picture of his multi-faceted heritage and draws attention to his claim to anglophone antecedents as well as to an Irish culture that is 'Other' but of equal merit.

Crucially, the most striking and distinctive feature of *Cynthia*, the *tensone*, or epistolary exchange, at the end of the text underscores its political dimensions and also reaffirms its Irish particularity. This structure is not found in contemporary English volumes from the 1590s, even though there had been greater emphasis on non-amatory themes and the depiction of male friendship in the mid-sixteenth century, as Cathy Shrank has shown.[67] The *tensone* was, above all, a feature of the early modern Italian and French sonnet.[68] Thus, in re-invigorating the Continental practice of using the sonnet for political debate, *Cynthia* advertises the breadth of learning of the author and foregrounds its kinship with the traditions of European humanism and its readiness to depart from the recent innovations and fixtures of English models. But more importantly, the incorporation of this epistolary exchange alerts us to the fact that dialogue amongst a group of informed male peers and the politicized knowingness of homo-social communication are as much anchors for the symbolic configurations of this sonnet sequence as the vagaries and unfolding drama of heterosexual love. The startling change of view effected by this shift of scene to a group of interlocutors who seem to mirror the author is

67 Cathy Shrank, '"Matters of love as of discourse": the English sonnet, 1560–1580', *Studies in Philology* 105 (2008), 30–49.

68 On the variable uses of the *tensone*, see Matteo Pedroni and Antonio Stäuble (eds), *Il genere "tensone" nelle letterature romanze delle origini* (Ravenna, 1999).

certainly amongst Nugent's most conspicuous alterations to the form which he evidently delights in refashioning. A final component in the subtle inflections and reorientation of the genre achieved by the poet, or possibly his posthumous editor, is, as already noted, the concluding announcement of the death of the author. The customary aspiration towards renunciation or sublimation in traditional sonnet sequences is hence given a new dimension here. The symbolic foreshadowing of the poet's demise in 'His leave taking of Cynthia, wherein his owne death is presaged' is unexpectedly literalized but immediately turned to aesthetic account. Closure is achieved through this sudden flourish. The death of the Irish sonneteer becomes a counter in the winningly persuasive argument posed in the final reckoning to Cynthia. Thus, the clumsy and dissonant closing lyric in Italian further adds to the unsettling and radical nature of this text which deftly reworks the poetic conventions which it also invokes and utilizes.

The epigraph to *Cynthia* is peculiarly apt and evocative. It also illustrates the intricate connections between Nugent's poem and its intertexts and the way in which they animate and add suggestive layers to its key conceits. The Latin in the quotation, it must be noted, is faulty suggesting that the author may have been relying on memory. Like the title of the sequence overall, which overtly draws attention to the 'direfull' emotions of the author, it gives peculiar prominence to unresolved emotional anguish.[69] However, it also implicitly underscores the heroic dimensions of such pain as the speaker is the Greek warrior, Heracles. The lines derive from Sophocles' play, *The Women of Trachis*. They are uttered by the dying Heracles who wrongly thinks that he has been wilfully murdered by his wife Deianeira who has sent him a poisoned garment. He proclaims that 'a woman, a female and unmanly in her nature, alone has brought me down, without a sword'.[70] In fact, his death is not an act of vengeance on the part of his wife but has been brought about in error as she tried to win him back from a rival. Heracles's speech castigating Deianeira is cited by Cicero in his *Tusculanae Disputationes*, a text that investigates the emotions, and advocates Stoic reserve and forbearance. The dying hero's quest for justice is of less moment to Cicero than his ability to bear pain and to face death unflinchingly. Heracles's accusation consequently is woven into a Ciceronian argument about the need to accommodate suffering. Hence

69 The word 'direfull' means dreadful or terrible. The *OED* gives its first occurrence as 1583. Nugent, in deploying this adjective, foregrounds the calamitous nature of the subject matter he is treating and also assigns a chillingly prophetic role to his text. Nicely, Nugent's direful sonnets anticipate the so-called 'terrible' or despairing sonnets composed by Gerard Manley Hopkins in Dublin in the late nineteenth century.

70 Sophocles, *Volume 2: Antigone, the women of Trachis, Philoctetes, Oedipus at Colonus*, ed. and trans. Hugh Lloyd-Jones (Cambridge, MA, 1994), pp 227–9. The Latin text that Nugent cites garbles these lines.

Nugent's epigraph is at once an appeal for justice and a fragmentary citation from a philosophical treatise that advocates strength and masculine endurance.

The dedicatory sonnet continues the theme of magnanimity in defeat in recounting the story of the vanquished Darius who accepts aid from a poor man who brings him a cup of water. The initial poems trace the growth of love and depict it as an overwhelming cosmic force that is nonetheless aberrant. As in the conventional associations of Petrarchan poetry, Cynthia's eyes paradoxically act as rival suns and so attract the attention of the poet. His love for her is likewise represented in the familiar feudal vocabulary of the sonnet tradition. Her impact on him unmans him and reduces him to 'groveling' (I.ii) on the ground. In the swift reversals that typify the volatile emotional transactions of Petrarchan desire, she immediately removes herself 'like the trembling Deere, of Hound afeard', thus changing his act of unquestioning obeisance into a transgression. Ovidian images of the moments of trespass that precede violent punishment and enforced transformation are regularly invoked by Nugent and constitute a prime symbolic nexus of his volume. The lover from the outset is cast in the role of Actaeon who is condemned for his furtive voyeurism when he spies on the chaste divinity Diana while she is bathing. This Ovidian figure is understood as falling prey to his self-consuming desires and being engorged by them. But he is also seen as an unwitting perpetrator who becomes a victim when he is turned into a deer and hunted either by his own hounds or those of Diana.[71] The sudden occlusion of the lover's world in Nugent's text, 'My Summers day ere noone was turned to night' (I.ii), suggests this dual dimension. The darkness intimates, not only the speaker's feelings of devastation and shame, but also the deleterious effects of a power who capriciously withdraws her favour and even goes so far as to treacherously turn on those she formerly supported.

The succeeding sonnets alternate between entreaty and accusation and between encomium and castigation, with the poet depicting himself variously as a self-effacing supplicant and as an angry, importunate lover who is asserting his rights. Cynthia is at once taken to task and determinedly pursued. Her absence and disregard force the lover into an impassioned assault on her and a defiant but despairing acceptance of his outcast role. The rupture caused by Cynthia's cruel spurning of her suitor is symbolically captured in the pointed irregularity of the third poem, which is an extended sonnet of eighteen non-rhyming lines. The fracturing of poetic decorum fittingly mirrors the disorder of an inadmissible love suit. In sum, the crisis of rejection at the beginning of the sequence becomes the very grounds for poetic ingenuity and the spur for the Irish poet's

71 On the varying dimensions of the myth of Diana and Actaeon, see Jonathan Bate, *Shakespeare and Ovid* (Oxford, 1993), pp 38–9, pp 45–7, pp 183–4 and pp 217–19.

self-fashioning. The ardent lover is compelled to assume a variety of poses and adopt multifarious guises in order to plead his case.

In particular, the sonnets emphasize a complex set of correlations between different forms of envisioning through the repetition of an aggregate of images linked with seeing, the reflective properties of water and imagining. In Sonnet iii, the 'dutious eyes' of the poet become a mirror or 'watery glasse' in which Cynthia may view herself. A parity between lover and beloved is implied here. Indeed, his status as tearful supplicant endows him with a moral righteousness that supercedes the transcendent authority of his divine mentor. Sonnet iv, in envisaging Cynthia as Leda, Danae and Daphne, enstates her as a chaste and put-upon maiden who evades male rapacity. Yet, the analogies are acknowledged to be imperfect as she falls short of such ideals of female probity since her heart does not 'conforme to her complexion' (I.iv). Sonnet v uses the conventions of the *carpe diem* theme and ominously foretells the decay of Cynthia's beauty and reminds her that she will, in old age, regret the effects of her actions. In construing these arguments, the author adverts not merely to the hortatory appeal of his rhetoric but also to its juridical force. In Sonnet v, his 'writings' are depicted as 'plainely' reinforcing his obvious 'right', while in Sonnet vi he represents himself as an opponent in war who will call off his siege in order to 'compound', that is come to terms with, his beloved – who is in part his rival – and arrive at a compromise or mutual concession.

The theme of temporality which has already been introduced in allusions to Cynthia's impending senescence and bodily decay is given further dramatic force in Sonnet viii. The allusion to the passage of 'foure gloomie Winters' renders the conventional accounts of the effects of time far less abstract. The elapsing of four years is also mentioned in the sestina that concludes the first part of the sequence in a detail that Nugent adds to the Petrarchan original which he is translating. Hence, the thwarted love that Nugent describes is at once particular and generic. It appears to be as much rooted in an historically specific occasion as in the universal dynamics of Petrarchism. Indeed, the arguments of the lover in *Cynthia* are given extra weight because they represent a special instance or case. The precise chronology of this broken romance hints at the historical particulars that determine and exert pressure upon this text.

Further, the exact computation of the time that has gone by since the beginning of this fateful love is one of the several elements that give dramatic structure to Nugent's carefully orchestrated volume. *Cynthia* is marked by that struggle between narrative and lyric that Heather Dubrow contends is a feature of many sonnet sequences.[72] The self-replicating patterns of Petrarchan discourse

72 Dubrow, *Echoes of desire*, pp 28–35 and 125–9.

in which the lover perennially lapses into despair, thus undermining any emotional advances that he may have made, are pitted in many sonnet collections against the desire for progression. Nugent's text is unusual because, while drawing upon the ritualized and repetitive affective designs of Renaissance love poetry, it also traces a discernible trajectory by plotting the genesis, gradual attenuation and final triumphant reinstatement of his love. His frequent resort to *concatenatio*, that is the interlinking of poems through the repetition of the final line of one poem as the opening of the succeeding one, further reinforces this impetus to transform the blockages of the political and amatory exchanges of the sonnet into a medium for tactical negotiation and philosophical insight.[73]

The eloquence that is one of the chief weapons of the Petrarchan poet is frequently cancelled out by his sense of impotence. The persuasive power of his writing is contrasted with the muteness that overwhelms him in actuality. Even his work at times lacks purchase because it is ultimately a vehicle of a privatized interiority that is inherently inexpressible. Sonnet vii hence ends with an account of the 'woes' of the poet that 'are so great I cannot showe them'. Sonnet ix makes explicit why Nugent's subject matter presents him with particular difficulties: Cynthia is a 'treasure that our Ireland hideth'. He momentarily wonders how Samuel Daniel, a fellow sonneteer and the author of *Delia*, might have described 'the wonder of our Isle', but convinces himself in the couplet that this local cynosure should never be disclosed or surrendered to an outside authority. Hence, Daniel is cited as a fellow-poet and his aid enlisted perhaps especially because the sonnets that he composed were valued for their directness and lack of embellishment.[74] However, Nugent's feelings of solidarity with his English peer are qualified by his recognition of the distinctiveness of his Irish material and viewpoint which need jealous guarding and necessitate a special discourse.

Sonnet xi by contrast is an address to Cupid, a recurrent figure in Sidney's *Astrophel and Stella*, and depicts the poet as having helplessly succumbed to his cruel regime. The final sonnets in the initial part of the sequence place increasing emphasis on the oxymoron of the 'cruell faire' and on the sense of oppression that the lover feels as a victim of Cynthia's power. In Sonnet xii, she has become his 'soules theefe', while Sonnets xv and xvi deploy vivid images of unnatural couplings, a white hind with a 'mongrell whelpe' and a hawk with a 'kestrell kite' respectively, to underscore Cynthia's treachery. This barbaric inter-

73 Dubrow notes that *concatenatio* is a striking feature of the sonnet sequences by Samuel Daniel and William Percy, but that it is rarely used by more canonical authors such as Sidney and Shakespeare. See Dubrow, *Echoes of desire*, p. 58.

74 For a discussion of Daniel's verse and the multiple revisions of *Delia*, see 'Introduction', Maurice Evans (ed.), *Elizabethan sonnets*. Revised by Roy J. Booth (1977; London, 1994), pp xxviii–xxxi.

mingling of species also suggests the infringement of the laws of decorum and the upturning of the privileges and responsibilities of class. Contrary to the customary perception that the female addressee of the Renaissance sonnet is always remote and silent, Cynthia moreover is given a voice in Sonnet xii and even has recourse to writing an avowal of love in the sand – 'my friend I will not thee forsake' – in Madrigal iii. In both cases, her protestations and promises prove to be empty.

Death and exile become intertwined as themes in the closing sonnets, thus prefiguring the predominant motifs of the second part of the sequence. The notion of 'soile' is given peculiar signficance in these parting meditations. The poet notes that he has spread Cynthia's fame 'in forraine soiles' in Sonnet xvii, while in The First Madrigall he conjures up a vision of bliss in which Cynthia is fully present and projected as walking in a stylized but consolatory pastoral landscape:

> Happie the lake wherein she bathes her face;
> Happie the soile ordain'd to be her place.
> Soile, lake, groue, flowers, to ease my deep distresse,
> Impart some part of your great happinesse.

The repetition of the term soil here alerts us to its carefully weighted resonance.[75] It is now not foreign but a vital component of a charged evocation of place. Indeed, there is an inkling, because of the reference to the lake, that the scene envisaged encapsulates aspects of the domestic terrain of the Irish midlands with which the poet was familiar.[76] Additionally, Cynthia in this projection of her is a pedestrian and earthly figure who is linked specifically to a locality and a native context. She is no longer an idealized or remote abstraction. The concluding sestina, a version of poem 22 in Petrarch's *Canzoniere*, is also deliberately chosen to continue this iconoclastic mood, as it momentarily conceives of the possibility of physical fulfillment while also deliberately foregrounding the further decline of the poet into despair. In addition, Nugent's utilization of this complex form counterpoints the recalcitrance of his subject matter with his mastery as poet. The sestina is made up of six six-line stanzas and a three-line *tornata* that reprises all the rhymes of the poem. The first stanza makes use of six different words in the end-rhyme position that are then repeated in varying locations in the five succeeding stanzas. This pattern known as a *retrogradatio cruciformis* has

75 In early modern English, soil variously meant earth or ground, land or country, or homeland. Nugent overlays these various meanings. See *OED* s.v. 'soil'.

76 For a description of the landscape and lakes of this part of Ireland, see *An introduction to the architectural heritage of County Westmeath* (Dublin, 2007), pp 5–7.

the effect of binding together potent forces in order to offset a spiritual decline. Nugent's poem depicts the dejection of the lover who is trapped in that amorous wood to which Virgil consigned those who die in love.[77] Yet, it ends with a wistful aubade in which the poet imagines retooling the Ovidian myth in such a way that Daphne does not flee from Phoebus but rather stays in his arms. The bitter recognition that he will die before such consolation be granted to him prepares us for the unremitting blackness that characterizes the second section of the volume.

Petrarchan lovers are customarily volatile and mood-driven. The unequal distribution of power between an autocratic and disdainful beloved and a subservient and emasculated lover, who yet seeks to press home his claims, leads to frequent abrupt changes of mood and tone. The speaker regularly alternates between hope, assertiveness and rage, while recrimination and invective are as much features of the addresses to the mistress as eulogy and declarations of devotion. Despite this established convention of swift and inexplicable emotional transitions, the programmatic darkening of tone at the opening of the second part of *Cynthia* is jolting and disturbing. The atmosphere becomes unrelentingly bleak and funereal as the poet's verses have turned in sonnet i into the 'abortiue brood of my deceased hopes'. Moreover, the themes of death and of the lover's suicidal despair, which had already been elaborated on in the first section of the sequence, are now startlingly interlinked with the desire for vengeance. The term 'revenge' is repeated twice in the opening sonnet and remains a leitmotif of the interwoven lyrics in this portion of the volume. The demand for violent redress far exceeds the querulousness of the traditional Petrarchan suitor and plays a pronounced and even overdetermined role in the pathological melancholia of Nugent's projection of embattled love.

Despair is conceived of in allegorical terms in sonnet ii. The lover, akin to Edmund Spenser's Red Cross Knight, visits the 'mansion of dispaire' and is further encouraged by this self-defeating personification to perpetuate his disaffected state.[78] His unjust victimization by Cynthia is the subject of the succeeding poems in which she is depicted as a ravenous 'Vulture' (II.iv), the baneful moon that induces lunacy (II.v) and as a fickle but unyielding maiden (II.vi). Poetry further is deployed as a form of meta-commentary as the text self-consciously reflects on its own status and powers. The pastoral landscape of love intermittently invoked in the first section of the poem is now endowed with a forensic function. In sonnet iii, the poet calls on the trees and lake in which he

77 On the sestina, see Petrarch, *Canzoniere*, p. 531. For the 'mourning fields' of the lovelorn, see Virgil, *Aeneid*, VI.440–76 , vol. 1, trans. by H.R. Fairclough and revised by G.P. Goold (Cambridge, MA, 1999).

78 See Edmund Spenser, *The faerie queene*, ed. A.C. Hamilton (London, 2001), I.ix.33–54.

has inscribed his love to plead his cause and also to articulate the injustice that he has suffered:

> And you tall trees, my loues true monuments,
> Retaine those lines which in your coates I carved
> That men her name may read, and reading hate,
> That was in love so false and so ingrate (II.iii).

If Nugent could conceive of an affinity between his poetry and that of Samuel Daniel in I.ix, in II.vi he realizes how much separates him from Philip Sidney who was able in his *Arcadia* to contrive a happy ending for his hero, Musidorus. The latter figure, unlike the protagonist of *Cynthia*, succeeded after many misadventures in winning back his beloved Pamela from a lowly rival.[79]

Despite this unabating strain of despair, the self-renewing, albeit debilitating, nature of love is depicted in the central lyrics of part two. In sonnet vii, love, phoenix-like, is rekindled by its own flames, while in sonnet viii the poet's 'love and truth' are represented as elemental forces whose powers of expression compensate for his mute hopelessness. Indeed, poetry is shown to give voice to truths that are censored or suppressed in the social sphere. In sonnets ix and x, the poet tries to rein in his 'inuective Muse' or mitigate her mournfulness, but is forced to recognize that his outspoken verse will at least indemnify the sincerity of his love after his death. The *canzone* that follows these texts is a curious composite, as it translates segments of poems 325 and 332 of Petrarch's *Canzoniere* and fuses them with a representation of the triumph of Cupid. The latter aspect of this lyric is reminiscent of allegorical portrayals of love as a pyschomachia, such as the besieging of the Castle of Jealousy in *Le Roman de la Rose* or Britomart's penetration of the House of Busirane in *The faerie queene*.[80] Unlike in a Petrarchan *canzone* which is usually a philosophical meditation on the metaphysical value of love, Nugent's poem aspires to be a dramatization in another vein of the lover's oppression. He becomes the victim of a belligerent Cupid who malevolently attacks him by striking him through the heart with an

79 Musidorus, however, is a vexed hero. He is narrowly prevented from raping Pamela by the arrival of bandits and is arraigned with his comrade Pyrocles at the end of the text for the murder of Basilius, king of Arcadia. See Sir Philip Sidney, *The countess of Pembroke's Arcadia*, ed. Maurice Evans (London, 1977). The complex intertextual links with the *Arcadia* adumbrate but diplomatically gloss over the conflicts between the Nugents and Sir Henry Sidney during his terms as Lord Deputy of Ireland.

80 See 'The assault on the castle', Guillaume de Lorris and Jean de Meun, *The romance of the rose*, trans. Charles Dahlberg (1971; Princeton, NJ, 1995), pp 179–215 and *The faerie queene*, III. xi–xii.

arrow. At the end of the lyric, however, he tries to turn this unjust assault to his advantage by urging this destructive deity to avenge the wrongs done to love by targeting Cynthia and bringing her to account.

The madrigals that follow the canzone starkly revisit the scene of the poet's humiliation and reinforce his sense of desolation. In Madrigal i he is overcome by the beauty of Cynthia only to be crushed anew by her scornful glance, and in Madrigal ii he repeats his determination to bid farewell to life. This reassertion of the core dramatic moments of Nugent's narrative, the cruelty of the beloved and the ensuing suicidal despair of the lover, however, is a prelude to an unexpected deviation from the traditional endings of the sonnet sequence. In a departure from the irresolution that is frequently the only closure that can be proffered by volumes of Petrarchan love poetry, the poet in sonnet xi laments not only his rejection by Cynthia but also his banishment by her from his native country. In suddenly asserting the theme of displacement and evincing an embryonic nationalism, Nugent's text not only intersects with the predominant motifs of the Irish bardic traditions with which he would have been conversant but also with the preoccupations of several Renaissance sonnet sequences such as Joachim du Bellay's *Les Regrets*.[81] His beautifully wrought lyric on the pain of exile thoroughly reconfigures the amatory struggle at the heart of his complex volume and with a flourish illumines it from a wholly different perspective:

Fare-well sweete Isle, within whose pleasant Bowres
I first received life, and liuing ayre;
Fare-well the soile, where grew those heau'nly flowres
Which brauely decke the face of my fierce faire;
Fare-well the place, whence I beheld the towres
With pale aspect, where her I saw repaire;
Fare-well ye floods, encreased by those showres
Wherewith mine eyes did entertaine despaire;
Fare-well cleare lake, which of art made the glasse
To rarest beautie, of mine ill the roote,
When she vouchsafes vpon thy shores to passe,
Blessing thy happie sand with thy faire foote;
Farewell faire Cynthia, whose unkind consent
Hath caus'd mine euerlasting banishment.

81 See Joachim Du Bellay, *The regrets with the antiquities of Rome, three Latin elegies, and the defense and enrichment of the French language: a bilingual edition*, ed. and trans. Richard Helgerson (Philadelphia, 2006). In the *Regrets*, du Bellay drops the device of the Petrarchan mistress and concentrates instead on his feelings of loss and nostalgic recollections of France while in exile in Rome.

The register of loss is entirely recalibrated in this affecting sonnet with its sixfold leave-takings and plangent enumeration of the occasions of 'farewell'. Instructively, the poet's eroticized longings centre now on a beloved homeland ('sweete isle') and locality ('soile') rather than on an unyielding inamorata. The studied Petrarchan gamesmanship of unrealized desire has become inextricably bound up with an equally visceral and tragic scenario: that of political exile and dispossession. Cynthia too is transmuted in this dramatic recasting of the fundamental metaphors and circumstances that inform the poem. She is at once envisaged as an unreachable heavenly ideal, an Irish *genius locii* and an errant ruler who enters into misguided pacts and imposes palpably unjust sentences on her subjects.

The elusive and shape-shifting narrative subtending Nugent's text is further reformulated in the interchanges of the closing poem, 'His leave taking of Cynthia, wherein his owne death is presaged'. In this sonnet, the departure of the poet is depicted as an enforced but voluntary exile contrary to its earlier representation as a harsh legal decree:

> Comming to take my last leave of my Loue,
> (Oh that I then leaue of my life had taken,)
> I told her how I now my chance would proue
> Abrode, since home-borne hopes had me forsaken.

The balance of power has perceptibly altered as the poet tries to assert control over his own fate while yet continuing to protest his loyalty. The notion of exile remains politically charged, but it is now portrayed as a potent weapon that can be wielded to advantage by the disenfranchised. Strikingly, too, in a conspicuous remoulding of convention, Cynthia is subject to an unexpected volte-face. Instead of sustaining the stony obduracy of the uncaring Petrarchan mistress, she undergoes a sudden transformation and capitulates, at least in part, to her interlocutor's arguments. She volubly pleads with her suitor and pityingly empathizes with his fate, lamenting the fact that when he dies he will lie 'lowly earthed, in an uncouth land'. In a deftly executed exchange of roles, the poet in this ironic final confrontation adamantly maintains a dignified silence on the grounds of his wounded honour, while Cynthia assumes, in lieu, the burden of immoderate passion typical of the Petrarchan lover by anguishedly deploring his fate and decrying the horror of exile.

Even though the term 'Finis' draws a line under the second part of *Cynthia*, Nugent appends a third segment to his poem which, as in all his subtle modifications of the sonnet tradition, succeeds in confounding expectations and further drawing attention to the craftsmanship and distinctiveness of his creation. This section, despite appearing to be an afterthought or casual epilogue, significantly and purposefully alters the tenor and import of the entire volume. It mischievously upends what we have read thus far and forces us to re-engage in new ways with the principal tropes that have been deployed. Additionally, it explicitly advertizes the Irish grounding of the text and situates it in a particular social and political milieu, that of the younger scions of some of the leading Old English families in the Pale in the late sixteenth century. Above all, its insouciance notwithstanding, this final part of the poem foregrounds its self-conscious artifice and gestures towards the obscured political undercurrents of the sequence as a whole. Here, text in effect cedes to meta-text; the pathological and destructive duologue of the poet and his beloved is abandoned in favour of a sustaining, many-sided and witty conversation between male friends.

The *tensone*, or epistolary exchange, consists of six sonnets circulated between the author, Richard Nugent of Dunower, William Talbot and Thomas Shelton. Their attempts to disabuse the the poet of his feelings and to prove to him that his love is nothing more than lust have the effect of strengthening his resolve and reviving his ardour rather than undermining it. The badinage of this male coterie is followed by a philosophical meditation advocating a retreat from public life and the embrace of pastoral existence. A final text in Italian, which almost offhandedly announces the death of the poet, presages that Cynthia's suffering will be allayed in the afterlife. A closing vision of transcendence thus cancels out the devastating and darkly rendered conflicts portrayed throughout the volume. Cynthia is offered the prospect of entry into a heavenly community – amongst which the poet is numbered – as a respite from the unhappiness of her mortal condition. With finesse, a reconciliation between the warring parties of the poem is negotiated and effected. A poetic sublation of the political and emotional dissensions that had formed the substance of the amatory sonnets is ultimately achieved.

The superaddition of the *tensone* to his sonnet sequence allows Nugent to harness the political vigour and originary force of the *dolce stil nuovi* writers such as Dante and Guido Cavalcanti who wrote such poems of correspondence. In the frank exchanges with Richard Nugent of Dunower and William Talbot, the primary tropes of the poem are subject to scrutiny. They especially question the meaning of love and threaten to unmask the figure of Cynthia as an illusion or an emanation merely of the author's desire. The epistolary exchange, moreover, seemingly provides an insight into the origins of the poem in a manuscript culture as it either mirrors or mimics the manner in which poetry is produced and passed around by a coterie and acts as a cement for an intimate and discrete social group.[82]

82 For an important investigation of the formative role of the coterie in verse production in early

Above all, this third part of Nugent's text adverts to its embeddedness in a specifically Irish social world and underscores, not only a native facility with and ready ownership of a pan-European literary tradition, but also the extent to which poetic conventions are remodelled and take on peculiar resonances when adapted to a particular national setting.

V: READING 'CYNTHIA' POLITICALLY

Although Richard Nugent's choice of the designation 'Cynthia' for his beloved follows convention in electing for a name that foregrounds her ideality, it is also deliberately motivated.[83] The figures of Cynthia and Diana were indelibly associated in the period with Elizabeth I in her identity as imperial goddess and the embodiment of virtue, probity and justice. A rich array of attributes linked variously with Astraea, Cynthia, Diana, Belphoebe and the Virgin Mary were melded in iconographic portrayals of the queen. The aim of such depictions was to allay fears about femininity and power and to produce sacral images of royal authority in an era in which the monarchy began to assume absolutist dimensions. As recent commentary has shown, however, what Frances Yates once dubbed 'the cult of Elizabeth' was less an immutable set of ideological impositions than a fluid series of negotiations between subject and ruler which did not preclude critique.[84] It is striking, moreover, that the iconic image of Elizabeth as Diana came under particular pressure in the representations of New English Planters and adventurers in Ireland. Edmund Spenser's multiple refractions of the monarch as Una, Belphoebe, Britomart, Mercilla and Diana in *The faerie queene*

modern Ireland, see Andrew Carpenter, 'Circulating ideas: coteries, groups and the circulation of verse in English in early modern Ireland' in Martin Fanning and Raymond Gillespie (eds), *Print culture and intellectual life in Ireland, 1660–1941: essays in honour of Michael Adams* (Dublin, 2006), pp 1–23. Carpenter sees the final part of *Cynthia* as indicating the existence of a cohesive literary group of which Nugent was a member (pp 8–9). The possibility remains, however, that all these poems are composed by Nugent alone and that he is projecting this many-voiced discourse.

83 Few poets make use of this name. The homoerotic sonnet sequence by Richard Barnfield (1574–1627) is entitled *Cynthia with certaine sonnets and the legend of Cassandra* (London, 1595) and Alexander Craig (1567?–1627) calls one of the eight women Cynthia to whom he addresses sonnets in his *Amorose songes, sonets and elegies* (London, 1606). The Roman poet Sextus Propertius also wrote a text entitled *Cynthia* that depicted the tribulations of love and the fickleness of his mistress.

84 See Frances A. Yates, *Astraea: the imperial theme in the sixteenth century* (London, 1975), Helen Hackett, *Virgin mother, maiden queen: Queen Elizabeth and the cult of the Virgin Mary* (London, 1994) and Louis Adrian Montrose, *The subject of Elizabeth: authority, gender and representation* (Chicago, 2006).

create a complex account of female virtue, while Walter Ralegh's poetic fragment, *Ocean to Scinthia,* depicts the poet as the cruelly abandoned lover of his fickle ruler.[85]

In projecting an Irish beloved whose name is Cynthia, Nugent effects a daring and multi-layered appropriation of this conceit. By recasting this figure as Irish, he is re-situating and making his own of the amatory poetics of the Elizabethan court. She is simultaneously the Virgin Queen and an unnamed Irish woman who is a member of the intimate familial interconnections of the Old English community of the Pale and the subject of his passion. Throughout the text, she hovers ambiguously between these rival associations. On one level, in declaring his tormented but undeviating love, the poet enunciates his loyalty to Cynthia, the English monarch, but also exposes her abuse and neglect of her subjects in Ireland. On another level, he recasts the malleable trope of the love for a sacral and all-defining female power and uses it to outline the lineaments of an Old English identity. His bond with Cynthia bespeaks his attachment to locality, involvement in the networks of power of the Irish Pale, investment in Gaelic culture and rootedness in the landscape of Westmeath. Subtly, the figure of a Diana-like ruler is commuted from an icon of imperial power into a symbol of Irish national belonging. She becomes indeed an archipelagic totem. Through his fluctuating and unstable relations with Cynthia, Nugent establishes those forms of social distinction that characterize the threatened community of which he is a member, and also delicately articulates the sentient or emotionally contoured nationalism of this grouping.[86] Its code of honour, loyalty, fear of displacement, urbanity, warrior ethos and wounded pride are obliquely captured in the manifold sexual disputes and erotic entreaties of the succeeding poems. The felt vicissitudes of Petrarchan love become the means by which the difference of Old English identity can be registered. Equally, it may be mooted that the divisions portrayed in the text poetically transpose not only the increasing conflicts between Anglo-Ireland and the English regime but also the internal dissensions within the war-torn, violent and rivalrous social world to which Nugent belonged.

In his eloquent meditation on Garcilasco de la Vega's pioneering sonnets, composed in the fortress of Goleta near Carthage in 1534 while fighting in the

85 Agnes Latham (ed.), *The poems of Sir Walter Raleigh* (London, 1951). In his dedicatory sonnet to Ralegh in the 1590 edition of *The faerie queene* (p. 733) Spenser particularly associates the figure of 'Cinthia' with this writer.

86 Christopher Warley persuasively contends that sonnet sequences are concerned with accruing social capital and establishing markers of distinction and difference. See *Sonnet sequences and social distinction in Renaissance England* (Cambridge, 2005). On the notion of a sentient nationalism, see Anthony D. Smith, '"Set in the silver sea": English national identity and European integration', *Nations and Nationalism* 12:3 (2006), 433–52 (p. 438) and Christopher Highley, *Catholics writing the nation in early modern Britain and Ireland* (Cambridge, 2008), pp 1–22.

service of Charles V on Spanish imperial campaigns in North Africa, Richard Helgerson argues that their power resides in their ability to open up the split between empire and love. He further notes that certain jostling forces characterize the new poetry that is produced throughout Renaissance Europe, basing itself on Italian and French models: it is propelled by a longing for transformation and renewal; it depicts a fatal loss of self in the pursuit of desires that run counter to political ambitions; and it evinces a commitment to place and to male friendship. Helgerson's evaluation of the dynamic but often countervailing energies sustaining the vernacular poetry of sixteenth-century Spain is also applicable to Nugent's *Cynthia.* This work connects with the universalist structures of the early modern sonnet sequence and inventively responds to the multiple challenges of this demanding form. It is fuelled by a desire for transformation and innovation as evidenced by its dexterous reworking of inherited conventions. It articulates with a new-found intensity the grief caused by the severance from a cherished homeland and the prospect of exile, but as a counterweight elaborates on the formative love for a native place and cultural milieu, the pleasure of male collaboration and friendship and the value of the supportive networks of a diasporic Catholic community. Moreover, its transformation of a Petrarchan love sequence into a bardic poem of exile and a politicized epistolary exchange advertises its multi-ethnic origins and the varying cultural contexts – amongst them Gaelic Ireland, the anglophone Pale, Renaissance England and Counter-Reformation Europe – which define it. However, its stark rendering of the suicidal melancholia, vengeful compulsions and the devastating self-alienation of the poet-lover underscores the inveterate social and political struggles in which this text is implicated.

With remarkable *sprezzatura*, the ending of *Cynthia* succeeds in effecting a symbolic concord which was never a possibility in the political realm. Nugent's slim but skilfully orchestrated and finely attuned volume imagines a future for the Old English community in Ireland which was never to be realized. As the crisis-ridden and strained affectivity of *Cynthia* also prophetically registers, the gap between empire and love, between the Tudor colonial ethos with its insistence on cultural and religious uniformity and the split loyalties, tribalism and pluralist cultural affiliations of the Old English families in Ireland, was, in the course of the seventeenth century, to widen rather than to diminish.

87 Richard Helgerson, *A sonnet from Carthage: Garcilasco de la Vega and the new poetry of sixteenth-century Europe* (Philadelphia, 2007).

A note on the text

There are two extant copies of *Cynthia*: one in the Huntington Library in California and the other in the British Library in London. The copy text for this edition is the British Library text.

My editorial practice had been guided by an intention to present the modern reader with a text that is as faithful as possible to the printed original whilst still being intelligible. Therefore the original spelling, capitalization and italicization have been retained and in cases where the seventeenth-century spelling may cloud the meaning an explanatory footnote has been provided. There are four exceptions: (1) the word 'then' has been changed to 'than' when it is used as a comparative (2) first-word capitalization at the beginning of a line has been regularized throughout (3) contractions have been expanded and (4) the numbering of each of the poems has been regularized. Some regularization of punctuation has been carried out silently.

Angelina Lynch
Dublin, May 2009

CYNTHIA

O multa dictu grauia: perpe u aspera.
Que exantlato corpore atq; animo pertuli
Feminea vi, femineo interimor vultu.[1]

R. N.

1 The epigraph, in garbled Latin, derives from the speech in Sophocles' *Trachiniae* in which the dying Heracles castigates his wife Deianeira whom he wrongly believes to have murdered him. The speech is cited by Cicero in his *Tusculanae Disputationes*.

The Dedication of this *Booke*. To the right honourable the Ladie of *Trymlestowne*.[1]

Ladie most worthy, of most estimation,
In whome all goodnesse is together knit;
Whose vertues purchase fame, fame admiration,
Of holyest will ioyn'd with a heau'nly wit;
Whose praise, if I would shew by word, or writ,
(A Theame too hye for Ciceroes *Oration)*
My words from my thoughts reach as low would flet[2]
As my thoughts reach from so high contemplation.
Receiue in gree this ill agreeing matter,[3]
An idle worke in idle houres dispatcht.
The Persian *King, whose power the world did threat,*
Tooke in good worth a poore mans cup of water;[4]
Who needes not scorne a whit to be thus matcht,
If to be good, be more than to be great.

1 Catherine Nugent, daughter of Christopher Nugent, Baron of Devlin, had been the baroness of Trimelston. She died ten years before the poem's publication.
2 reach = capacity for comprehension (*OED* n.[1] 6a); flet (fleet?) = to drift (in the air), (*OED*, II, 3). Lines 7–8 may be paraphrased: My words (of praise) 'flet' low beneath my 'thoughts reach' (my comprehension of her) which in turn falls short of 'so high contemplation' (the object of contemplation – the baroness herself).
3 in gree = in goodwill.
4 A reference to the Persian king, Darius III (*c.*380–330 BC) who was defeated by Alexander the Great of Macedon at Issues in 333 BC and at Guagamela in 331 BC. Whilst fleeing Alexander, Darius was deposed and arrested by the Persian nobleman Bessus. Darius was mortally wounded by his captors and was left to be found by an advancing Macedonian soldier who was said to have offered him a cup of water before he died.

THE FIRST PART

Sonnet I

The Planet, whose swift course diuides the times
And warmes the earth, that she her burden yelds,[1]
Approached now vnto our northerne clymes,
Leauing the scorched *Æthiopian* felds;[2]
The birds that in that seazon still rejoyce
To see their wythred bowers new clad with greene,
Did summon me, in their sweet warbling voice,
To giue attendance on the Summers Queene.
I straight obeyd, and by two Christall streames
That through a pleasant groue forth murmering slide,
I layd me downe, and viewd bright *Phoebus* beames,
Which mounted from the East with glistring pride.
But soone my minde and lookes from thence allured[3]
Two Sonnes whose light had *Phoebus* light obscured.[4]

Sonnet II

Two Sonnes whose light had *Phoebus* light obscured,
Firing with their bright beams the neighbour brooks,
Mine eyes with wonder and delight allured
Upon themselues to bend their curious looks;
When loe, I spide a Nimph of peerelesse beautie,
In whose white face those planets faire were fixed,
To whome in lowly wise I did my dutie,
Of feare and reverent loue together mixed;

1 burden = produce of the land; yelds [yields] = produces.
2 felds = fields.
3 allured = were drawn to.
4 Two Sonnes (suns): a reference to his beloved's eyes. Phoebus = the god of the Sun, also known as Apollo.

But she, my fainting voice no sooner heard,
And saw where on the ground I groueling lay,
Then like the trembling Deere, of Hound afeard,
Backe through the shadey grove she hyed away:
Away she hyed, and when I lost her sight,
My Summers day ere noone was turnd to night.

Sonnet III

My Summers day ere noone was turn'd to night,
And now no light frequents my darkesome bower,
For since that houre that my fair *Cynthiaes*[5] eyes
Did mine surprise with their diuine aspect,
Yet no respect would haue to my reliefe,[6]
Blacke nights of griefe succeed my Summers day.
    O beautious *May*, so may thy beautie flourish,
The Heauen so nourish;[7] may thy blooming floures
And fertile showes raine downe of happinesse
Still still to blesse thy dayes; as thou wilt deine
To rew my paine, and sound my woes retreat,[8]
That growes so great because thou grow'st so beautious.
    Look on those dutious eyes; behold, alas,
The watry glasse where thou thy selfe mayst view,
And let that hew that first procur'd my paine[9]
Dart forth againe those comfortable beames
To dry these streames which drowned haue my rest.
A small request is one relenting looke.

5 Cynthia is an epithet for Artemis, the Greek goddess of hunting and virginity (equivalent to the Roman Diana). It was also a common term of poetic address for Elizabeth I.
6 Yet they [Cynthia's eyes] would give no consideration to my relief.
7 So that your beauty may flourish, Heaven nourishes it.
8 rew [rue] = regret.
9 hew [hue] = face (*OED*, n.[1], 2).

Sonnet IV

Where in the Store-house of the heau'ns was found
The goodly sampler, whereout nature wrought[10]
That fair embraudrie which exceeds mans thought,
As farre as doe the stares our retch from ground.[11]
Faire *Læda*, whose rare beautie so renownd,
Great *Iove*, from his celestiall seat downe brought,
When he the Warders of that treasure sought
To tempt with showres of gold, as bookes resownd;[12]
Nor *Daphne*, in her hunteresse aray,
Walking in the woods the day that *Phoebus* chast her,[13]
Could euer threds of so pure gould display,
Nor such vnspotted mynes of Alabaster.
And were her heart conforme to her complexion,
Our earth had not envyed the heau'ns perfection.

Sonnet V

Cynthia, the time will come when looking backe
Thou shalt behold how time hath tryed my truth,[14]
And proudly tryumph'd in thy beauties wracke;
(Too late for both of vs) thou wilt have ruth,[15]
And grieue that thou diddest not in time betake
Thy selfe to that from which thou now so swaruest,

10 whereout = from which.

11 retch = reach.

12 The poet appears to be confusing the story of Leda with that of Danae, daughter of King Acrisius of Argos. According to Greek myth, the king had been warned that a future son of Danae would be responsible for his death; consequently he kept his daughter imprisoned so that she would not become pregnant. However Zeus (Jove) entered the prison as a shower of gold and impregnated her. Cf. Sidney, *Astrophil and Stella*, Sonnet VI.

13 In Greek mythology Daphne was a nymph who lived and hunted in the forest. She eschewed lovers and fled from the God Apollo (Phoebus) when he pursued her. On praying to be delivered from his attentions she was transformed into a laurel tree.

14 tried = proved.

15 have ruth = take pity.

When blasts of age thy youthes faire fields doe shake,
Which were not reap'd in season of their haruest.
Regard (deere Mayd) my right, so plainely show'd
In these my writings, by thy name adorned,
And thinke thy blooming youth there best bestow'd
Where thy declyning age shall least be scorned.
So harmes foreseene are better still preuented
Than by experience of the losse repented.

Sonnet VI

Long haue I sought (O ruthlesse faire) to scale[16]
The long resisting walles of thy disdaine:
Th' assaulters were sighes, teares and visage pale,
Which outwardly bewrayd mine inward paine.
Desire conueyd this ruth-deseruing rout[17]
Vnto the fort where my best hopes are seated;
But then thy threatening frownes straight sallyed out,
And with their might the weaker force defeated;
Yet loth thus recreant to forsake the field,
Behold, how fairely to compound I proffer;
Choose thy conditions as thou list and yeeld,
And for reward see here what I doe offer:
The purest love, that ever heart did hold,
More worth than Mountaines of the *Indian* gold.

Sonnet VII

Here, *Cynthia*, at thy feet I humbly tender
The keyes of my (till now) vnconquered heart,
Whence I sue forth, voyd of affected art,
Sighes, teares and prayers to make my soules surrender.

16 faire (fair) = a beautiful woman.
17 ruth = pity; rout = troop.

Thou art a woman, women should be tender,
Shew by thy sentence of what sex thou art,
And let their humble sutes preuaile in part
That plead not for an obstinate offender.
All seeke to breake thy brests congealed Ice,
But so hard is thy heart that nothing mooues thee;
Ah leaue, deere Loue, to be henceforth so nice,
The onely fault for which the world reprooues thee,
And weigh not lightly so his sound advice,
That with such faith, such truth, such feruor loues thee.

Sonnet VIII

Cynthia, the teares which frõ mine eies down flowing
Did represent the Spring-tides of my sorrow
Are now quite spent; eu'n when my cares new growing
Had greatest need their further aid to borrow.
My voice, which had in charge my teares to second,
Is with incessant cries grow'n hoarse and broken;
For now foure gloomie Winters hath it reckon'd,
Since of my love to thee it first had spoken.
Then, since my teares and voice at once are reft me,
View in my face the dumbe shewes of my greefe;
Read in these lines, which onely now are left me,
Legions of woes raunged in words so briefe.
Sure they would move thee if thou once did'st know them,
But, ah, they are so great I cannot showe them.

Sonnet IX

Oft haue I wished, in my zeales excesse,
To make my *Cynthia* see proofes of my dutie;
That in these lines I could as well expresse
As in my soule I doe admire her beautie;[18]

18 i.e. that my poem can express her beauty as strongly as my soul admires it.

Or that great *Daniell*, fit for such as taske,[19]
This wonder of our Isle had seene and heeded,
Then should his glorious muse her worth vnmaske,
And he himselfe, himselfe should haue exceeded;
Then England, Fraunce, Spaine, Greece and Italye,
And all that th' Ocean from our shoares diuideth,
Would over-runne their bounds, and hether flye
To finde the treasure that our Ireland hideth.
But best is that we neuer doe disclose it,
Since knowne but of our selues we shall not lose it.

Sonnet X

To thee, the Lodestone of my heauie thought,
To thee, the Starre that guides my beaten barke,
To thee, the fairest one that nature wrought,
To thee, that art the worlds admired marke,
I send these mournfull hymnes my zeale hath brought
From out my lightlesse griefs *Cimmerian* darke,[20]
And from dispaires deepe gulfe that long hath sought
To drowne thy glorious praise in my liues Arke.
Appease (ô louely Mayd) this raging storme
With thy sweet smiles, to me more comfortable
Than his *Ermoes* to the Sea-mans eies.[21]
What though mine artlesse lines want phrase and forme,
Thy fauours may their lowlinesse enable
To lift thy sacred name aboue the skies.

Sonnet XI

Cupid, that under thy sweet Yoke hast brought
Th' inhabitants of this huge globe around,

19 A reference to the poet Samuel Daniel (*c.*1562–1619) whose work includes the sonnet sequence *Delia* (1592).

20 In Greek myth the Cimmerians were people who lived in perpetual darkness, near the land of the dead.

21 Ermoes = St Elmo: a naturally occurring light that appears around a ship's mast, usually during bad weather.

And that the depth of my desires do'st sound,
And seest the secrets of mine inward thought.
Thou seest, I feele, how deerely I haue bought
My wayting on thy standerd so renownd,
And yet thou leau'st me groueling on the grownd,
By long delayes now tir'd and ouer wrought.
I see, but too farre off, that lamping light[22]
To which thou doest me driue, and spurre amaine,
But lo, I want thy wings to make my flight;
Enough, and more, doe my desires obtaine,
If I may wast in my desires by leyser,[23]
And that my sighes and teares do not displease her.

Sonnet XII[24]

I saw in earth a forme Angelicall,
And heau'nly graces in a worldly wight,[25]
Which did my soule so rauish and delight,
That since her name I celebrate and call.
I sawe from her faire eies the teares downe fall,
Those eyes which oft haue dim'd the Sunnes cleare light,
And heard her sighing, vtter words of might
To stay the flouds, and moue the mountains tall.
Doole, pittie, anger, worthinesse and loue,[26]
So sweete a mourning melodie consorted,
That thither woods, and hills, and rockes remove,
And dead mens bones out of their grave resorted.
The spheares and stares did stray from their due course,
Such of this heau'nly musicke was the force.

22 lamping = beaming (*OED*).

23 Wast (waste) = to become weak / enfeebled; by leyser (by leisure) = slowly / by degrees (*OED* 5. c). The poet wishes to waste away gradually and hopes that his tears and sighs do not displease his mistress.

24 Cf. Petrarch, *Canzoniere*, 156.

25 wight = human creature.

26 doole = grief.

Sonnet XIII

Mine eies, how can you without dazeling view[27]
The fairest hew that euer eie had seen?
That souereigne Queen whom your sad looks have sewd,[28]
No Sunne hath vewd nor neuer shall her peere.
O you more cleare than are the sunnes cleare beames,
Receiue these streames, the tribute of mine eies.
And you my cries, the orators of sadnesse,
Turning my gladnesse into ruthful moanes,
Ioyne with my groanes, blacke registers of sorrow,
And sad words borrow of my dolefull tongue
To tell the wrong that you bereeues your food;[29]
Then what sowre moode can moue her to withstand you.
So fairly land you in that happie port,[30]
Where doth resort the prize for which ye venter,
And lowly enter to complaine my grief
To my soules theefe, my liues Judge now ordained.
Let mine vnfeigned faith preuaile, deare iewell,
O be not cruell since thou art so faire.

Sonnet XIV

O be not cruell since thou art so faire,
Let not disdaine my high deserts disgrace,[31]
Nor one foule fault thy beauties prize impair,
Sweete thoughts do best beseeme so sweet a face.
Behold the triple region of the aire,
Woods, valleys, mountains, rocks and euerie place
Are filled with Ecchoes of my plaints and prayer,
Which at thy deaffened eares still sue for grace.
All of them shew, each in his diverse kind,

27 dazeling (dazzling) = the condition of being dazzled (*OED*).

28 sewd [sown] = strewn.

29 bereeves (bereave) = to snatch away / deprive (*OED*). The sense seems to be: 'Words from my grieving tongue will express the pain that robs that tongue of its food, i.e. appetite'.

30 The poet continues to address himself.

31 desert = a meritorious deed or action (*OED* n[1], 2b).

That of my wofull case they haue compassion;
The rocks my words repeating seeme enclin'd
To beare some burden of my hidden passion.
Ah *Cynthia*, heare at length my grieuous mones,
And be not harder than these senseless stones.

Sonnet XV

When careful thoughts that long disturb'd my mind
Had giu'n my wearie sences leaue to rest,
Old *Morpheus* arose as beetle blinde,[32]
And did with his blacke Mace mine eyes arrest.
Me thought I saw a louely milke-white Hind,[33]
Whom straight pursued a stately Hart whose crest[34]
Did well declare he was of noble kind,
And fawning shew'd he lou'd the gentle beast;
Then forthwith did a mongrell whelpe appeare,
His Sire a Stag but on a Roe begotten,[35]
And soone this noble Hart beheld his deare
Accept th' vnkindly beast, himselfe forgotten,
Who thence-forth euer raung'd the fields alone,
And to the woods and winds still made his mone.

Sonnet XVI

Unto the woods and winds he made his mone,
And sure his dolefull case I greatly rued,
But that my mind was call'd from thence anone,
To heed as strange a sight that straight ensued.
Me thought two gentle Hawkes, but ioind in one,

32 Morpheus is the god of sleep who was thought to induce dreams.
33 Hind = a mature female deer of the red deer species
34 Hart = a mature male deer of the red deer species.
35 Roe = a small species of deer which Nugent contrasts with the Stag or Hart and the Hind (the presumably more noble species of red deer). See *OED*. The 'mongrell whelpe' is a product of miscegenation and is therefore unworthy of the Hind's affection.

By kind and kindly choice aloft I viewd:
When lo, I saw the female soard and gone,
After a kestrell Kite, obscurely mewd;[36]
Which sight so sore my fantasie did vexe,
That suddenly I start out of my slumber;
Not *Cynthia* but the frailtie of her sexe,
Doth me with sad suspect and feares encumber;
But ere my deere, my Hawke, make such a flight,
O let these eyes first want their wonted light.[37]

Sonnet XVII

O let these eies first want their woonted light,
And vgly death my captiue corps immure,[38]
And day be cancel'd by eternall night,
And no Sun-shine, nor Moone, ne stars endure
Ere the worlds wonder and my soules delight,[39]
Which doth the stares downe from their seates allure
To yeeld their homage to her beautie bright
Should her faire worthes with so foule staines obscure;
Ere I, who blaz'd her name in forraine soiles,
Making old *Albion* shores her praise resound,
Should see a stranger triumph in my spoiles,
Or any else with my fresh garland crown'd.
No, no, those Planets that her birth allotted,
Will neuer see their glories glasse so spotted.

Sonnet XVIII

O dismald dreames, offspring of sleepe and night,
Hels messenger fore-telling our misfortune,
Robbers of rest and enemies of light,
That still with hastie sights our sence importune.

36 mewd (mewed) = feathered (*OED*, a[1]).
37 want = to lack; wonted = customary (*OED*). The poet wishes for death.
38 immure = imprison / confine (*OED*).
39 Ere = rather than.

Could not my *Genius*, ill affected spright,[40]
Contriue the ruine of my weake estate,
But you, O cursed dreames, for more despight,
Must before time mine ill prognosticate?
And thou, that hast my loue so meanly prized,
The hire[41] thereof vnto a straunger giuing;
Was it for this I thee haue canonized
A heauenly saint, though here on earth yet liuing?
Ay me, what crosse iniurious starre assign'd
So faire a face to such a faithlesse mind?

Sonnet XIX

Like as the siluer swanne in her extreames
Be-mones her selfe with doolefull harmonie,[42]
And takes her last leaue of her haunted streames,
Assuring them that now her death drawes nie,
So thou, my Muse, breath out in dying notes
The sad discourses of my heauie fate,
And let thy lines yclad in mourning cotes,
My neere approaching end prognosticate;
And thou, poore heart, sometime the blissefull bowre
Where louely *Cynthia* deigned to repose her,
Thy ioyfull tunes change into wailing sowre,
For now thy ioy is past and thou must loose her.
Yet with thy wracke procure in her some ruth,
And make the world admire such loue and truth.

Madrigal I

Happie the beautious flowers and herbars soote,[43]
Wherein my *Cynthia* with the Muses walkes;

40 According to classical belief, a genius was a spirit allotted to each person at his birth to govern his fate.

41 hire = reward.

42 The swan was said to sing before she died. The poet is also referred to as a swan ('cigno') in the final sonnet, written in Italian, of the sequence.

43 herbar = harbour: a place of retreat for wild animals (*OED* n[1], 2.c.); soote = sweet.

Happie the shore that heares her as she talkes,
And beares th'impression of her daintie foote;
Happie the groue which her aspect doth grace;
Happie the lake wherein she bathes her face;
Happie the soile ordain'd to be her place.
Soile, lake, groue, flowers, to ease my deep distresse,
Impart some part of your great happinesse.

Madrigal II

The wounded deare from running never ceaseth,
Spur'd by the piercing shaft within his side;
His grieuous paine doth him still forward guide,
And still his restlesse race his paine increaseth.[44]
Right so fare I with that same deadly dart,
Wherewith fierce loue hath pierc'd my conquer'd hart,[45]
The more I flee, the more my wound doth smart.
And now I find in vaine they flee or tarrie,
That with themselves their owne destruction carrie.

Madrigal III

One day as I attended on that Saint,
To whom my sighes and teares I sacrifice,
She sate besides a lake and cast her eyes
On me, who then renew'd mine old complaint,
And from the strond a slender reede did take,[46]
And wrote: my friend I will not thee forsake,
Vntill that mount be covered with this lake.
I list not of my *Cynthia* stand deciding,[47]
But feare the sand whereon she wrote was sliding.

44 These lines echo the story of Actaeon related in book three of Ovid's *Metamorphoses*. Actaeon spied on the virgin nymph Phoebe whilst she bathed in the woods and, as punishment, was transformed into a deer by Diana, whereupon he was torn to pieces by his hounds.
45 A play on words: hart = a male deer.
46 strond = the edge of a lake.
47 i.e. I do not wish to stand in judgement over Cynthia.

Madrigal IV

Sweete are my *Cynthiaes* smiles, and comfortable,
As are the Sun-beames in a clowdie morne,
That turne to glistering ore the nights dim sable;
Or as his presence who in *Ouids* fable,
We read, was on the Eagles wing vpborne
To heau'n, that might serve at *Ioues* high table.[48]
Faine would I leave unto the world instable,
Some monument of mine intier affection,[49]
And of her pow'r that holdes me in subiection;
But since my stile is for this taske vnable,
My silence shall admire her perfection.

Madrigal V

Vouchsafe but once into my breast to looke,
My breast where thy disdaignes deepe wounds have dinted;
There shalt thou read thy worthes as in a booke,
And mine affections force at large imprinted.
This table made the world at first acquainted
With thy faire forme therein so liuely painted;
This is the shrine where thou alone art sainted.
Destroy not then sweete *Cynthia* with disdaignes,
The shrine that thee, and nought saue thee containes.

Ballata[50]

The fire which I suppos'd had beene extinct
By those cold winds which her disdaignes forth blew,
Enflames, torments and wounds my heart anew

48 In the tenth book of *Metamorphoses* Ovid relates the story of Ganymede, son of the king of Troy, who was so beautiful that Jove took on the form of an eagle and carried him off to the heavens to be his cup-bearer.

49 intier = unfeigned / sincere (*OED*, 10).

50 Cf. Petrarch, *Canzoniere*, 55.

That now too well I find it was not spent,
But rak'd in imbers pale to feed it still,[51]
And so reserued for a worse intent.
Mine eies, that brakish teares so largely spill,
As Limbecks serue, through which doth aye distill[52]
The griefe that me consumes, which if they knew,
The Indian Tygres could not choose but rue.
What fire so furious but would soone be quencht
By those huge waues that walter from mine eies,[53]
If loue my walles about had not entrench'd;
Who with such art these contraries applies,
And so besets each passage with his spies,
That when I thinke I doe his snares eschew,
I find me rauish't with her heauenly hew.

Sestina, *translated out of* Petrarc.[54]

To every beast that harbroughs here on earth,
Except some few which may not brooke the Sunne,
The time of trauell is the cheerefull day;
But after when the heau'ns alight their starres
Some hie them home, some stay them in the wood
To rest their wearie lims against the morne.
And I when once appeares the Christall morne
To chase grim darknesse from about the earth,
Waking the sillie beasts in euerie wood,
Haue neuer truce from sighing with the sunne;
And after when I see the kindled starres,
I waile and weepe and eft desire the day.
When sable Eu'n exiles the gladsome day,
And our blacke night lends forreigne shores the morne,
I pensiuely behold the cruell starres
That hath me fram'd ay me of feeling earth,

51 imbers = embers.

52 limbeck = a distillation device: the poet's eyes are like limbecks as they distill his grief into tears; aye = continually (*OED* adv. 1a).

53 walter = flow / gush.

54 A translation of poem 22 from Petrarch's *Canzoniere*.

And curse the day when first I saw that Sunne,
Which makes me looke like one nurst in the wood.
So fierce a Tygre in the wildest wood
Did never feed as yet by night ne day,
As shee for whom I weepe by shade and Sunne,
Gaining no truce from teares at eu'n ne morne;
And though my self be made of lowest earth,
My high desires come from the loftie starres.
O that ere I returne to you faire stares,
Or to my wonted walkes within the wood,
Tyring this corps which soone will turne to earth,
I saw her rue me, who may in one day,
Repaire my foure yeares losse, and ere the morne[55]
Enrich me at the rising of the Sunne.
That I were with her at the set of Sunne,
And none beheld vs saue the silent starres,
One night that could be shortened by no morne,
And that she might not turne into greene wood
To leaue mine armes *as Daphne* did that day
That golden *Pheobus* chas'd her here on earth.[56]
But first shall earth enclose me in the wood,
And dayes gray cope embrodered be with starres,
Before my Sunne enjoy so sweet a morne.

FINIS

55 The reference to 'four years' is an embellishment by Nugent; it is not contained in Petrarch's poem.

56 See note 13.

THE SECOND PART

Sonnet I

Step forth into the world mine Orphane verse,
Abortiue brood of my deceased hopes,
And doolefully pursue your parents hearse,[1]
Attir'd in your blacke stoales and tawnie copes.
Such mourning weedes beseemes our mournfull woes,
And sith reuenge is all your remedie,[2]
With out-cries loud to coasts vnknowne disclose
The dire contriuer of my tragidie.
Then prophesie with holie furie fir'd,
And tell faire *Cynthia* how the heau'ns on hie,
The sunne, the stares, the earth haue all conspir'd
To wreake my wrongs and end her tyrannie;
And that the sprights below and pow'rs aboue her
Threaten reuenge for murther of her louer.

Sonnet II

Led by the fainting steps of folorne hope,
Onward I go, where froward fates me driue,[3]
Till past the bounds of this our Horoscope
With wearied lims at last I did arriue
Within a desert, darke, vnhaunted caue,[4]
So low that loath'd it seem'd of worlds pure aire;
And by the Poesies on the posts ygraue
I found it was the mansion of dispaire.
Further I past vnto an inner roome,
Where that sad wight sat crosse-leg'd in his chaire,[5]

1 Cf. Walter Raleigh, *Scinthia*: 'but my loves wounds, my fancy in the hearse / the Idea but restinge, of a wasted mind', 11–12.
2 sith = seeing that … ; remedie (remedy) = reparation (*OED*, 2a).
3 froward = unfavourable / perverse.
4 desert = deserted / forsaken.
5 wight = a thing personified (*OED*, 2b): in this case the poet's despair.

And humbly pray'd him to vnfold his doome,
If any blisse my bale should aye repaire.[6]
Die wretch, quoth he, and leaue not Fortunes scorne;
Thy hap was burned ere thy hopes were borne.[7]

Sonnet III

Faire trees, in whose smooth rines I oft engrau'd[8]
That name which loue had in my heart enrold;
To whom as in those burning fits I rau'd,
My neuer ceasing paines at large I told.
Cleare lake, whose calme vast floore I ouer-pau'd
With teares that from my fertile eyes downe rol'd,
When of your waters oft I humbly crau'd
To ease my flaming bowels with their cold:
Declare my foure yeares love, my discontents,
And how I haue at *Cynthiaes* hand deserued.
And you tall trees, my loues true monuments,
Retaine those lines which in your coates I carued[9]
That men her name may read, and reading hate,
That was in love so false and so ingrate.

Sonnet IV

O that my loue were with thy liking ended,
And with thy faith my fire had also turned,
Thy fault should not thus still be reprehended,
And few had know'n the flame wherein I burned.

6 bale = misery / grief (*OED* n[1], I, 3).
7 hap = fortune / lot.
8 rines (rinds) = bark.
9 Cf. Ronsard, *Sonnets pour Hélène*: 'Voux ruisseaux, voux rochers , vous antres solitaires / Vous chesnes, heritiers du silence des bois / Entendez les souspirs de ma derniere vois / Et de mon testament soyez presents notaries / Spoyez de mon mal-heur fideles secretaries / Gravez-le en vostre escorce …' [Streams, rocks, caves lone, and oaks, the legatees / of silence in the woods, since I have spent / of all my sighs the last, green notaries / seal with your leaves a lover's testament. / Serve me as clerks, and scribble, ancient trees / my sorrows on your bark ...], 18, 218, 1–6. Translation by Humbert Wolfe (London, 1934).

My free-borne rimes that, ah, too long have mourned,
And from blacke *Lethes* gulfe thy name defended,[10]
Should of their charge thy praise be now disburdned,
And thou remaine unknow'n and uncommended.
But since my cruell stares decrees are such
As cause me loue and prosecute my death,
My constant end shall trie my loues pure tuch,
Yeelding the farewell of my failing breath
To thee, O Vulture on my heart-strings seasing,
Sith that my death is most vnto thy pleasing.[11]

Sonnet V

Maruell not, *Cynthia*, that my muse brings forth
These bitter fruits of long conceal'd disdaigne,
Seeking to taint thy neuer-matched worth
With oft obiecting thine vnkindnesse staine;
For all are rauings of a feeble braine
Of one whom love and hate haue long held sicke;
Who, weakened by the force of former paine,
By *Cynthiaes* change is wexen lunatike.[12]
Thou, *Cynthia*, art the Moone whose influence
The flowing tides of mine affects doth sunder;
Whose faire aspect, food of my greedie sence,
Now hauing lost I sterve; nor is it wonder
That my soules pow'rs thus from their Cels haue ranged,
Sith thou thy faith but not thy forme hast changed.[13]

Sonnet VI

Ay me, dispaire comes now to claime the scope
Of my sad thoughts drownd in deepe woes excesse,

10 In classical mythology the Lethe (meaning forgetfulness) is one of the five rivers of the underworld. Its waters were associated with oblivion and were said to induce forgetfulness.

11 sith that = so.

12 wexen = (wax) = become.

13 sith = seeing that.

For I am reft the object of my hope,
And my fierce faire a stranger doth possesse.
Yet *Sydneys* gentle sheepheard could deuise
In such a case to find a remedie,
Who blear'd his iealous hosts mistrustfull eyes
By his kind hostesse handsome industrie;[14]
Then why should I despaire of like successe,
Whose happie riual is a harmelesse boy.
But ah, my *Cynthia* doth this hope suppresse,
Who chastely proud persists and sweetly coy;[15]
But *Cynthia*, why do I for this reproue thee,
Since for thou wast so chast I first did louve thee.

Sonnet VII

The peerlesse bird bred in the *Arabian* soile,[16]
That solely lives on earth without a mate,
Strangely prouides by his owne finall spoile
An heire that may succeed him in his state;
For when he knoweth his houre he mounts so hie
That kindled by the sunne in flames he flashes,
And in that instant out begins to flie
An other of his kinde, borne of his ashes.
Eu'n so my heart consum'd with raging fire
Dies (*Cynthia*) that thy will may be fulfilled,
But straight loue charmes it with more fresh desires,
And so reuiues what thy disdeigne erst killed:
Thus doest thou kill, and cure againe, O cruell,
Because my flames may neuer want their fuell.

14 Most likely a reference to the prince Musidorus, a character from Sidney's *Arcadia*. Musidorus disguises himself as a shepherd in order to win the heart of the princess Pamela who has been removed from court to a rural lodge by her father in order to avoid an oracle's prophesy. Pamela is under the guardianship of the boorish Dametas whom Musidorus tricks in order to stage an elopement.

15 i.e. Cynthia's chaste pride and sweet coyness suppress the hopes of her suitors.

16 A reference to the phoenix, a mythological Arabian bird. When the phoenix died, a new phoenix was said to rise from the ashes of the funeral pyre of its predecessor.

Sonnet VIII

Those scalding sighes, which shew'd my harts chast fire
More hot than sunne-beames in the midst of Iulie;
Nor those warme teares sprung from more warme desires,
That on my ruthlesse love did wait so duly,
Could vnto that supreame reward aspire
An infant late hath got, start vp but newly;[17]
Whose birth or owne desert was nothing hier,[18]
Ne could his age yet learne to loue so truly.
Yet though I see my selfe thus made a scoffe,
I can not stoppe the course of my zeales flood;
My love and truth when hopes are all cut off
Shall grow like impes, which from hew'n stumps do bud.[19]
The world shall see, when nought my hope doth nourish,
My faith once vow'd amidst despaire can flourish.

Sonnet IX

Oh whither runst thou thus mine angry pen?
Whither my bitter and respectlesse rimes?
Gainst her who makes you loue in after times,
and summons you from out dumbe silence den.
O, how I shame the world abroad should ken
Your railing Satires, hates harsh sounding chimes,
So falsly charging with injurious crimes
The worlds chiefe wonder, glorie vnto men.
My soule, the pray to tyrannizing loue,[20]
Sound the retreat to mine inuective Muse;
Who though my ruthlesse faire thou canst not moue,
Must yet obey thy fate which sends the newes
That when my bones in earth are cold and rotten,
Thy flame shall not be quencht, nor love forgotten.

17 The syntax here is obscure but the sense seems to be: my tears that 'did wait' on Cynthia, could not aspire to the 'supreame reward' of her love as it has already been 'got' by an 'infant' (a younger man), an occurrence which has caused his tears to 'start up' again.
18 desert = worth / merit (*OED* n[1], 1b); hier = higher.
19 impes (imp) = sapling / scion.
20 pray = prey.

Sonnet X

Cease mournfull Muse thine unregarded mones,
That with my griefe encrease my loues disdaigne:
Disdaigne more hard to breake than marble stones
For those are pierc'd with drops of softest raine;
But I, that from mine eyes such showres do raigne
To mollifie a heart more hard than stones,
Find for my last reliefe but sterne disdaigne,
Which sutes my new-born griefs with new found mones.
Since then such griefe clad in such artlesse truth
In my remorseless faire no pittie sturres;
Since my complaints which must procure some ruth
In strangers eares do sound so harsh in hurs.
Ile silent die, and leaue to deathes recital
The storie of my love, and loves requitall.

Canzone[21]

The ruler of this mightie Monarchie,
That in his thought this triple frame sustaines,[22]
Ruling it after his diuine election,
Commaunded once the heau'ns and starres on hie
And Elements to joyne their pow're and paines
To build a worke of exquisite perfection.[23]
They straight their Lords direction
Obey with care and dutious diligence.
In such obedient strife they all contended
That soone the work was ended:
So stately, faire and of such excellence
As earst was never seene of mortall sense.
        The walles were built of spotlesse Alabaster;[24]
The roofe, wherein the owner seemed lauish,
Was all thicke couer'd with the purest gold

21 Cf. Petrarch, Canzone 325.

22 A reference to the classical / Christian belief in a tripartite universe divided into the celestial, terrestrial and sub-terrestrial spheres.

23 i.e. Cynthia.

24 walles (walls) = Cynthia's body.

Saue onely that the front white snow did plaister;[25]
The loftie windowes, that my soule did rauish[26]
With deare delight as I did them behold,
(Ay me that was so bold),
Were two blacke orbes encloz'd in circles blew
Of Jet and Saphire quaintly interlaced,
Which *Hebene* Arkes imbraced;[27]
Whence forth in troupes Loues winged souldiers flew,
And tooke me ere I could their waites eschew.[28]
The gate was built of snow-white Iuorie,[29]
All drawne in compasse curiously about,
And eu'nly set within pure Corall bounds;
The leaues were brazill of Vermilion die.[30]
Within a Porter sate who still sent out
A heau'nly consort of melodious sounds
Which gave me many wounds,
And cured them eft with *Balsamus* of ioyes;[31]
Not *Orpheus* song, ne Mermaids musicke rare,[32]
Could ever yet compare
With this delightfull, strange, melodious noyse
Which ends and breeds a new mine old annoyes.[33]
Amid the hall, there was a stately seate,
With curious skill and skillfull care ycarued:
A squared stone, of orient Diamond.[34]
Here reason sate, and great affaires did treat,
And with his lore this peerlesse worke preserued
Prescribing lawes vnto that happie land.

25 front = forehead.
26 i.e. Cynthia's eyes.
27 Hebene = ebony; Arkes = arcs; imbraced (embrace) = enclose / encircle. A reference to Cynthia's eyebrows.
28 waite (wait) = ambush (*OED*, I.1f).
29 i.e. Cynthia's mouth / teeth.
30 The 'leaues' refer to Cynthia's lips. brazil [brazill] = brazil-wood, a brownish-red wood from which red dye was obtained.
31 eft = afterwards; Balsamus (balsam) = a resinous medical preparation for soothing pain.
32 In classical mythology Orpheus was a poet and musician of great skill.
33 annoyes (annoy) = troubles / vexations.
34 Cynthia's brain. According to Greek medicine the higher mind, the seat of reason and objectivity, was seated in the brain whereas the lower mind, associated with emotion, was seated in the heart.

Loue walked on the strand,
For this faire pile is walled with fairest riuers,
And when he had espied the pleasing marke
He straight did bend his Arke,[35]
And at the precious Chaire he shot whole quiuers,
But ay the stone return'd his shafts in shiuers.
When thus a while in vaine his force he tri'd,
Scorning the shamefull foile he wheeles about[36]
T'awreake his spite vpon some weaker pow'r,[37]
And me vnarm'd alas he first espi'd
As I stood warelesse gazing in the rout,[38]
Which came to wonder at this goodly towre.
He star'd with visage sowre,
And from his quiuer tooke a golden flight,[39]
That from the rest of purpose he selected,
And when I least suspected
I felt the shaft full in my bosome light,
And yeeld I must that wanted force to fight.
Like one that hauing a repulse sustain'd
Assaulting of a fort, doth turne his way
And sacks some village weake and vnprepar'd;
Or like a Lion fierce with famine straign'd
Who, when he failes of his desired pray,
Deuoures the beasts which he before had spar'd:
So loue with me hath far'd.
But *Cupid*, if thy power which earst did vanquish
Bright *Phoebus*, thundring *Iove* and warlike *Mars*
Be not decayd and scarce,
With those bright armes that cause me thus to languish
Reuenge thine owne reproch, and ease mine anguish.
My song if any seeke
By their prompt wits thy mysteries to measure,
Let them diuine but never know thy treasure.

35 Arke = bow.
36 foile (foil) = defeat / repulse.
37 awreake (awreak) = avenge.
38 wareless = unwary / incautious.
39 flight = arrow.

Madrigal I

I saw my faire abrode the fields once randoning,[40]
That faire on whom the heau'ns their graces lauished,
Like louely *Thetis* her sea-bowres abandoning;[41]
My sprights forthwith with deepe delight were rauished.[42]
But then on me she cast her looke so scornfully
That downe I sunke, and she nought caring vanished,
And euer since I waile thus mournfully,
From my soules blisse by this dumbe sentence banished.
Then iudge the world how well my loue is guerdoned,[43]
Where I for meed request but to be pardoned.[44]

Madrigal II

The burning lampe, when once that oyle is spent
Whose humour erst preseru'd it in his prime,
Leeseth his light, and dieth incontinent:[45]
So I, whom falsehood and vnkindnesse rife
Haue left depriu'd of her who was sometime
Oile of my flaming lampe, lampe of my light,
Do bid my last adue to worldly ioyes.
Which I (God wot) have not enioy'd but seldome;[46]
For now mine end will end all mine annoyes,
And to a loathsome life faire death is welcome.

40 abrode (abroad) = outside; randon = to fly/move about at random (*OED*, 2).
41 In classical mythology Thetis was a sea nymph who was married to the mortal king Peleus. Peleus had to wrestle with Thetis as she changed into the forms of various beasts in order to win her.
42 sprights = spirits.
43 guerdoned = rewarded.
44 meed = recompense.
45 leeseth = loses.
46 wot = knows.

Sonnet XI

Fare-well sweete Isle, within whose pleasant Bowres[47]
I first received life, and liuing ayre;
Fare-well the soile, where grew those heau'nly flowres
Which brauely decke the face of my fierce faire;
Fare-well the place, whence I beheld the towres
With pale aspect, where her I saw repaire;
Fare-well ye floods, encreased by those showres
Wherewith mine eyes did entertaine despaire;
Fare-well cleare lake, which of art made the glasse
To rarest beautie, of mine ill the roote,
When she vouchsafes vpon thy shores to passe,
Blessing thy happie sand with thy faire foote;[48]
Farewell faire *Cynthia*, whose unkind consent
Hath caus'd mine euerlasting banishment.

Sonnet XII

You that peruse these sorrow charming rimes,
The dolefull ditties of a dying spright,
Vouchsafe to rue my ruth-deseruing plight,
And know the treasure of your happie times.
No glorie I affect of future times,
Such honours are too high for my poore plight:
Strive they for such whose vnaffected spright
Forge them a subject to set forth their rimes.
If any chaunce to find in these my rimes,
The liuely patterne of his deadly plight,
Let him condole with mine afflicted spright,
Whose griefe may not be told in length of times.
Times are too so short to shew my woefull plight,
No rymes can sound the sorrowes of my spright.

47 Cf. William Nugent, *Diombáidh triall ó thulchaibh Fáil*: 'Glan a locha's a linnte / aoibhinn álainn firminnte / a's tarbhach toir gach dhoire ...' (Her lakes and pools are clear. Pleasant and delightful is the sky, and fruitful the trees of every grove ...). Translated by Gerard Murphy in 'Poems of Exile by Uilliam Nuinseann Mac Barúin Dealbhna', *Éigse* 6 (1945–52), 11–13.

48 '... with thy faire foot': most likely a misprint of 'with her faire foot'.

Sonnet XIII

His leave taking of Cynthia, *wherein his owne death is presaged.*

Comming to take my last leave of my Loue,
(Oh that I then leaue of my life had taken,)
I told her how I now my chance would proue
Abrode, since home-borne hopes had me forsaken.
She then, in whom my piercing griefe did waken
Some sparke of ruth too late, alas, assayes
To crosse this course which I had vndertaken.
Now she perswades, now weepes, now sweetly prayes.
But, neither reasons, teares, nor prayers could raise
The siege that honour to my heart had layd,
When with a deep-fetcht sigh, the louely Maid,
The horror of her breast thus out bewrayes:
Wo worth, quoth she, must that deare head and hand[49]
Lie lowly earthed, in an vncouth land.

FINIS

49 Wo[e] worth = Alas!

THE THIRD PART

Sonnet I

To his Cosin Master Richard Nugent of Donower[1]

Mine owne *Dicke Nugent*, if thou list to know,
The cause that makes me shun my westerne home,
And how my tedious time I here bestow,
Where angry *Thetis* gainst her bounds doth fome;[2]
Weet that to ease that neuer-healing wound,[3]
Which now foure sommers heate hath made to fester,
By time, by absence, or by counsell sound,
I flee the soile where my sweete foe doth rest her.
I soiourne here where I remaine so easde,
By this my flight of the tormenting blow,
As doth the deare on whom the shaft hath seazde
By late vnbending of the deadly bow.
And since I haue this cursse eu'n fatall proued,
That I am borne to loue, and not be loued.

Sonnet II

The answer of M. Richard Nugent of Donower

Mine owne deare Dicke, whom I loue as my life,
And euer shall whiles I in life remaine,
I thee aduise to leaue this lingring strife
Betweene thy loue and thy loues hope so vaine;
And for those yeares wasted so long in vaine
To shed some teares with full remorse of minde,
And to be rid of thy tormenting paine,
To shun the path misguided by the blind.

1 Richard Nugent of Dunore was the chief landowner in the barony of Corkery, Co. Westmeath. He had been pardoned for his involvement in the 1581 uprising led by another of the poet's cousins, William Nugent. See Introduction.

2 bounds = boundaries; in this case the shore.

3 weet = to know.

As for to flee the place of thy decay,
I ne mislike, (if that may worke thine ease)
Yet better were this weed to roote away
Which so infects, and fils thee with disease.
For lust it is, not loue, that doth torment;
Where loue is just, there still is found content.

Sonnet III

A Reply to the former *Answere*

Deare is my Loue to me, as is my life,
And euer whiles I liue shall so remaine;
Ne can preuaile a whit thy friendly strife
Seeking to staunch my hearts loue-bleeding vaine.

Leaue then (deare Friend) thy words to waste in vaine,
Which so renew the affections of the minde;
My minde that proudly glories in my paine
Because it tels the world I am not blinde.

Ne can my Loue to those faire eyes decay,
Though their cleare beames did first my soule disease,
And rather will I still thus pine away
Than ransome with my loue, my loves hearts ease.
Pure is the loue which doth my life torment;
My life so well bestow'd, I die content.

Blaspheme no more against my Loue so iust;
Hearts truely loving cannot thinke on lust.

Sonnet IV

To his trustie Friend Maister William Talbot[4]

Now will I write to satisfie thy will,
Yet what thou least would read, that must I write;

4 It is impossible to identify William Talbot conclusively, but he was most likely a descendent or relation of William Talbot of Malahide – an ally of Nicholas Nugent.

For *Cynthia* breathes the Theame into my quill,
And what my hand layth downe shee doth endite.[5]

My will, saith shee, (O Wretch) is that thou liue,
And ever liue in neuer-dying griefe.
Hard dome,[6] which so denyeth that Tyrants giue
To haplesse wretches for their last reliefe.

This Theame I must delate and amplifie[7]
With tragicke Stories wrought by *Fortunes* spight;
How with one fatall blade both Lovers dye,
And of *Leander* drown'd in *Heroes* sight.[8]
Thus of the dead, I sad examples borowe
To furnish out a Scene of liuing sorrowe.

Faile not, my vowed service to commend
To that sweete Lady, in whom vertue shines,
Whom least I should her iudgement graue offend,
I leaue t'importune with myne idle Lines:
Fare-well & to thy trustie self retaine
These scencelesse rauings of a Loue-sick brayne.

Sonnet V

The answere of Master William Talbot

I will giue thanks for this thy great good will
That bind'st thy selfe at my request to write,
And well I like the subiect of thy quill,
Which in thy name my passions doth endite.
Well thou describ'st the state wherein I liue,
Nay how I die in euer-liuing griefe;

5 endite (indite) = to utter or suggest words that are to be written down.
6 i.e. doom.
7 delate = report / relate (*OED*, 5).
8 According to myth, Leander was a youth who was in love with Hero, a beautiful priestess of Aphrodite. Leander would swim to see Hero every night guided by a light in her tower, but one night a storm extinguished the light and he drowned. On hearing the news Hero threw herself into the sea.

And though thy woes to mine no help can give,
Yet fellowship to misers is reliefe.
Ioine then with me, thou need'st not amplifie
With aged tales thy wrong and Fortunes spite,
Since of like wounds we both at once must die,
And both our harmes procured by our sight;
Then write we still, and though thy lines I borrow,
Yet be assur'd I need not learne thy sorrow.

I neede not to that Ladie thee commend
With praise, who can decerne where vertue shines,
Yet did thine errand least I should offend.
Shee smil'd, perusing of our carelesse lines,
And say'd: write on, for if you should retaine
These idle humours they would breake your brain.

Sonnet VI

Maister Thomas Sheltons answer to the 4. Madrigall of the first part, which beginneth: Sweet are my *Cynthiaes.* &c.[9]

What wight saw captiue stile so comfortable
As that which thou didst send to me this morne;
Stile that t'enchant the gods themselves were able.
O that such rare conceipt should maske in sable,
Which ought with glorie crownd to be vpborne,
Unto the heavens, and plac'd at *Ioves* high table.[10]
Fortune, which euermore hath beene vnstable,
Enui'd thy vertues, and thy great perfection,
When she inchain'd thy heart in such subiection
Of one that is to pay thy loue vnable
With other thing than dumbe shewes of affection.

9 Thomas Shelton (1598–1629), a poet and the first translator of *Don Quixote* into English, was from a prominent Old English family. See Introduction.

10 See Part 1, note 26.

Sonnet VII

A Sonnet preferring the quiet life of the meane estate, to wealth and honors which procure enuie, and for the more part accompanied with danger.

Sweete is the life that clad in bare estate,
Farre from the reach of enuies hatefull sting,
Deuoid of malice, rancour and debate:
The chiefe attendants on the court and King;
Doth yet enjoy a quiet calme content
Estraunged from the pompe of Princes traine,
Vnto whose bow there may be found no bent,[11]
Ne bounds their high aspiring to containe.
Such was the blissfull life those sheepheards led,
Those harmlesse sheepheards that for loue so mourned;
Piping vnto their flock while that they fed
On the greene banks by *Flora* Queene adorned.
So happie liue they, though they live obscurely,
Who liue contented, quiet and securely.

A Sonnet in Italian, made in commendation of the Authour, and Perswading *Cynthia* to leave her sorrow.[12]

Cynthia quel cigno che di te canoro
Fe risuonar al mondo' l chiaro nome,
Lasciando in terra le terrene some.
Salit' al ciel canta nel' alto choro.
Il or choronate di celest' alloro
L'amato viso e quell' aurate chiome

11 bent of a bow = aim / intention (*OED*, bow, n1, 4c).

12 The swan was said to sing before it died and was thus associated with bards and poets. The poet addresses Cynthia, instructing her not to grieve. The Italian is garbled but an approximate paraphrase in English is provided; thanks are due to Francesca Bovone and Laura Pelaschiar for invaluable help with the translation.

Che le sue fiere voglie haueangia dome,
Invita al premio del mortal lavoro.
Il or sente tuoi sospir' e'l piant'e dice,
Non ti lagnar non ti guastar il viso
Che tosto finir ann' ituoi lamenti,
Sarai tu come noi anchor felice,
Alma gentil tra le beate menti
E bella piuche mai in Paradiso.

FINIS

[Cynthia, that swan that sang your clear name / Making it resound throughout the world /Has left on the earth its mortal remains /It ascended the sky and now sings in the heavenly choir /Now that its beloved face and golden hair/ Which its desires had already tamed/ Are crowned with celestial laurel / It invites (you?) to the prize of its mortal work / It now hears your sighs and crying, and tells you / Do not complain; do not spoil your face / Because soon your suffering will be over / And you will be happy again, just like us / A gentle soul amongst blessed mind / And more beautiful than ever in Paradise.]